Table of Contents

Introduction 3

The Art of Non-Verbal Communication..5

    Principles of Nonverbal Communication...16

    How to Improve Nonverbal Communication 17

    Functions of Nonverbal Communication..20

Understanding yourself and different personality types 25

    What do the dimensions' mean? 26

The Limbic Brain 39

    The Components of the Limbic Brain 40

        Amygdala...40

        Basal Ganglia 44

        Cingulate Gyrus 49

        Hippocampus..52

        Hypothalamus 55

        Thalamus 57

Full Body Non-Verbal Communication 60

    The Legs and Feet..61

    The Torso: chest, hips, and shoulders 65

    The Arms 69

    The Hands and Fingers 72

    Facial expressions..77

Avoiding Danger: Detecting deception 80

    Why is it difficult to detect deception through nonverbal behaviors?81

    Reasons why the identified nonverbal cues are not effective in detecting deception 83

How to be a Better Reader 91

    People are not as good as they think they are 92

    What are you doing wrong? 93

    Why is it important to know how to read people? 94

    Reading People 95

Bonding with people through body language 102

    Mirroring 102

        Creating the Right Vibes 104

        Mirroring on a Cellular Level 105

        Mirroring Differences Between Women and Men 106

        Looking Alike 107

        Steps to mirroring successfully 110

The secret to building charisma 114

Conclusion 122

Introduction

Nonverbal communication is a thing and it is very important to know how to understand it if you are to be able to fully understand what people are saying. Research has shown that most of what people communicate is done via nonverbal communications which is composed of body language, non-verbal cues and the likes.

Being able to analyse people and decode what they are truly saying beyond the words they use is a very useful skill for anybody to have especially if your job has to do with people. This will help you in convincing things to do those things you want them to do for the betterment of the human race among other things. Being able to speed read and analyse people will also be of great help during negotiations as it will help you analyse the person at the other end of the table, identify what it is they truly want such that you can offer it to them.

In the first chapter, you will learn about the different types of nonverbal communication that exists such as kinesics, complement, repetition, regulation, replace and haptics. You will learn about the different types of touch and what each means. You will also learn about the principles of nonverbal communication and how to improve your skills at communicating nonverbally.

In the second chapter, you will learn about the different personalities that exist and how to determine which is which. This will enable you to be better able to read what people are saying nonverbally.

Thereafter, you will be taught about the brain, the different sections that exist and the functions of each after which you will be taught about full body nonverbal communication.

You will also be taught about how to read people better, how to tell when someone is trying to lie to you as well as how to make friends of people by using no   nverbal communication skills. In all, this book is all encompassing as it provides in-depth knowledge of nonverbal communication that you won't find anywhere else.

Analysing people is a useful and indispensable life skill that will help any and everybody who knows how to do it move ahead in life. This e-book contains concrete techniques developed by psychologists that will enable you tell what is going on in another person's mind even if they are saying the exact opposite verbally. It will help you identify deceptive people, pick through the holes of people's stories and discover the truth for yourself. It is a book you will find very useful and which, once you go through it, will become a lifelong companion.

The Art of Non-Verbal Communication

Before you can be able to read people, you have to be able to communicate nonverbally. Understanding the nonverbal art of communication allows you to understand individuals better and communicate more effectively.

Nonverbal communication is essentially the process of sending messages and receiving them without the use of words either through writing or speaking. Nonverbal communication is also referred to as manual language. It is able to emphasize written languages in a manner similar to the use of italics in writing. In 1956, a psychiatrist by the name of Jurgen Ruesch and an author, Weldon Kees introduced the term "Nonverbal Communication" in a book titled "Nonverbal Communication Notes on the Visual Perception of Human Relations."

According to experts, a huge part of our communication is nonverbal as we respond to several thousand information using nonverbal cues and behaviors such as postures, the tone of voice, eye gaze, gestures and more. Virtually every aspect of our being ranging from our handshakes to our hairstyles and mannerisms can be used to reveal the kind of person we are, and also to impact the manner by which we relate to other people.

Nonverbal communication involves the use of signals that are often subtle such that it becomes difficult to be consciously aware of them. Several times, we communicate information in nonverbal ways by combining a number of behaviors such as frowning with the arms crossed and maintaining an unblinking eye gaze in order to indicate disapproval.

There are several types of nonverbal communication. They include:

Kinesics. Kinesics refer to the study of the way and manner with which we use body movements and facial expressions for communication. Several messages can be transmitted through the body movements, eye contact and facial expressions of an individual. Several people believe in their ability to interpret the message behind the facial expressions and body languages of others, however, the reality is different. It is found that it is almost impossible to interpret a particular gesture, facial expression etc., for the exact meaning intended by the individual who transmits them.

Despite this, humans rely heavily on kinesics in order to interpret facial expressions, gestures and express the meaning behind them. Kinesics are used in communicating like, social status, and even relational responsiveness. Facial expressions are regarded as a primary method for transmitting emotions and feelings.

Eye contact also plays an important role in nonverbal communication. It includes behaviors like looking, staring and blinking. When people come across things or people they like and approve of, the rate at which they blink increases and their pupils dilate. Also, when people look at one another, there is a range of emotions that can be interpreted from the look, ranging from interest to hostility and attraction.

Eye gaze is used in determining if an individual is honest or not. When steady eye contact is maintained between two persons, it is used to validate the person whose honesty is under scrutiny. It is a sign that the person is being truthful and is trustworthy. However, if the individual is shifty-eyed and is unable to keep eye contact, then the person is considered to be lying or deceptive.

An instance of facial expression is when you sit in a party at one end of the room and see someone that attracts you at the other end of the room. There are certain nonverbal behaviors that you are prone to receive and transmit before you can be able to ascertain if the individual is attracted to you. There are also certain nonverbal behaviors that you are going to be on the lookout for that will help you determine whether to go over and introduce yourself or not.

There are four distinct ways body movements reinforce your verbal messages:

Complement: body movements are able to complement your verbal messages by reinforcing the main idea. For example, you are providing an orientation to individuals as regards a software program. When you instruct an intern on a course of action to take by talking about it, you may thereby initiate the action. For instance, after telling the intern to click on a tab, you then click on it, thereby complementing your verbal message.

Repetition: you can also reinforce verbal messages by using nonverbal means to repeat the message. Using the example above, after you instruct the intern to click on a tab using verbal messages, you then make a motion to the right using your hand, the gesture in that context may suggest that the intern move the cursor to the tab. Repetition helps the listener to understand the message better.

Regulation: the use of body language helps to regulate conversations. For instance, if you nod your head during the orientation process with the intern, it indicates that you are paying attention, and it may encourage the interns to keep on asking questions. Holding your hand up with your palms out may be used to signal them to stop or pause, so you can answer their questions.

Replace: body language can be used to substitute or replace verbal messages. As mentioned earlier, it is found that facial features are used in communicating our feelings to other people, however, our body movements can be used in expressing the intensity with which the feelings and emotions are experienced. For example, if the facial expression of the individual indicates frustration during the process of using the software program, it means they need assistance, however, if they push the computer away and remove themselves from its vicinity physically, then, they are probably extremely frustrated.

Haptics: haptics refers to the study of touch. Touch happens to be the first type of nonverbal communication experienced as humans and it is essential to the development and health of human beings in general. Touch is used to indicate feelings and relational meanings. Hugs, kisses, and handshakes are used in demonstrating relational meanings and also to indicate relational closeness. Western society reserves touch essentially for romantic and family relationships. Generally, when females are involved in same-sex friendships, they are at more liberty to use touch in expressing their relationship than males in same-sex friendship.

However, despite these social norms, the need for touch is strong which is one of the reasons why men found ways to incorporate it into their friendship in a manner acceptable by society. One of these ways includes wrestling among young adults and adolescent males. Wrestling is regarded as a more socially acceptable way for men to touch each other as compared to the feminine way of hugging, touching one another, holding hands and so on.

This, however, does not indicate that males in western society are averse to touch. They shake hands in order to establish trust between themselves, shaking hands is also used to indicate agreement between two parties. They do touch but not at the same frequency and with the same intent females do. Touch between women is used to convey concern, nurturance, and care. Between men, however, it is used to assert control or power over others.

Cultural norms that surround touch and gender constructs are also responsible for preventing and limiting behaviors that might not be comfortable in society.

There are essentially five different types of touch.

Type of Touch	Example(s)
Functional-Professional Touch	Music teacher, Sports coach, Physical therapy, Medical examination
Friendship-Warmth Touch	Hug
Social-Polite Touch	Handshake
Love-Intimacy Touch	A kiss between romantic partners or family members
Sexual-Arousal Touch	Sexual caressing and Intercourse
Friendship-Warmth Touch	Hug

Personal Appearance, Objects, and Artifacts. These refer to the types of nonverbal communication used on our bodies and surroundings in order to communicate meaning to other people. They are used to represent self-concepts. Consider your choice of hairstyle, jewelry, clothing, automobiles, rings, and tattoos, as well as the way you take care of your body. The choices made are used to express meanings to the people around you concerning the things you value and the image you wish the world to see. As regards communicating, the choices we make concerning our personal appearance, artifacts and objects are usually within cultural contexts and whatever interpretation we make are in light of the contexts.

An example of this is the use of tattoos and its popularity today. Tattoos were at one time associated with prison and armed services, they have however become mainstream and are used to express a variety of messages relating to the person, politics, and culture.

Proxemics. Proxemics refers to the study of how our use of space influence the ways and manners with which we relate to other people. It is also used to express the kind of relational standing we have with the people around us. However, people essentially belong to different cultures and may, therefore, have different expectations for normative space. In a large urban area, it is practically inevitable to have people stand close to you, however, if you are from a rural area or culture where people expect the existence of more space, you may have someone stand "too" close for you to be comfortable. Proxemics deals with the space that exists between objects and people.

Proxemics is also often associated with social rank and it is an essential aspect of communicating in business. Such things as the owner of the corner office, the head of the table and who sits in it.

Edward Hall indicated that there are essentially two aspects of space – territory and personal space.

Territory: this aspect of space is related to control and it describes the way control is established over your own space. A young individual might claim his or her territory by painting it their favorite color or put up posters that reflect their own interest and the characteristics they find unique to themselves. Families mark their own territory by putting up walls or fences around their houses. One factor considered implicit in a territory is the sense of a right to control your own space. Territory refers to the space you claim as your own, you are responsible for it and you are willing to defend it.

Personal space: this aspect of space refers to the bubble of space that surrounds each individual. For example, when walking down a flight of stairs, we are prone to sticking to one side of the staircase for reasons best known to us. You may prefer sleeping on the right side of the bed, such that whenever someone else decides to sleep on that side, it may result in collusion. There are no lane markers in personal space and the bubbles of space that surrounds each person moves with them, thereby giving room for collusion.

The same Edward Hall also developed four categories of space used in forming and maintaining relationships.

Intimate Space: this consists of space that ranges from touch to about eighteen inches. This type of space is used with people we are close with such as family members, intimate partners, and close friends. Whenever violence and physical fighting ensues, this type of space is involved.

Personal space: this category includes space that ranges from eighteen inches to about four feet. This space is reserved for the majority of conversations that exists with non-intimate others which include friends and acquaintances.

Social Space: social space ranges from four feet to about twelve feet and it is involved in interactions among a small group such as sitting around a dinner table with other people, or a group meeting.

Public space: public space is the last category of space and it ranges from twelve feet and beyond. This type of space is most often used in situations that involve public speaking.

Space is used to regulate communication made verbally and also to communicate both social and relational meanings. In order to be able to better analyze people with regards to space, you could decide to go to a public space and observe people. Using the four categories, you can decide to group the people based on the amount of space between them.

Environment: the environment deals with the physical and psychological aspects of communication, they are nonverbal acts that transmit messages through the use of spaces we occupy such as our offices, cars, rooms, offices or homes. The environment is an important aspect of the process of communication, more than tables and chairs in an office. The way an individual perceives the environment he or she is in determines the way such individual will react to it. This type of nonverbal communication makes use of the meanings that others perceive about you based on the space you occupy and the meaning you try to send through the way you keep these spaces.

Most educational institutions choose to paint classrooms using dull colors in order to produce a calming effect on the students, thereby keeping them from being distracted by excessive stimuli and bright colors. Fast food restaurants, on the other hand, make use of bright colors and hard plastic tables and seats, in order to create an upbeat environment and make it uncomfortable enough to keep the patrons from staying longer than is necessary.

Google, for example, is famous for the environment where it conducts its work with spaces created for in-house food service around the clock and even physical activity. Although it is at a considerable expense, the actions of the company speak volumes. The result produced in an environment that is designed to facilitate creativity, collaboration and interaction is definitely worth the effort.

Chronemics: chronemics refers to the study of the manner with which people utilize time. The kind of attitude the individual develops towards time is also an important type of communication using nonverbal means. Does the individual arrive early for an event, right-on-time or late? How often does the individual arrive late or early to events? It is believed that the way we make use of time express a wide variety of meanings to the people around us. How would you describe an individual who is most frequently late? Then think about the individual who is the exact opposite of the first individual, i.e. How would you describe an individual who is always on time? How do you plan on describing the type of person they are based on the way they make use of time?

A high value is placed on being on time in the United States of America and more positive responses are offered individuals who are punctual in their endeavors. However, in several Arab and Latin American countries, the concept of time is used less strictly, and punctuality is not essentially a goal to achieve. When the expression "Indian time" is used, it refers to "the perception of time (that) is circular and flexible" (Harris, Shutiva). It is the belief that activities will begin when the gathering is complete and everyone is accounted for, and not according to a schedule that is determined by a clock or calendar. The different manners with which time is used can be employed in generating conflicts between individuals from different cultural groups.

In social contexts, time can be used to establish social status and power. Not many people like waiting, but you have to wait for people that are of a higher rank than you.

When a speech is presented, does your audience have to wait for you? Time is an important factor in the process of communication in your speech. The best way by which you can honor the audience is to respect the time expectation allotted to your speech

How long do you expect to wait for, after ordering a meal at a fast food restaurant? How long do you expect to wait for after ordering for a pizza online, before it is delivered to you? Essentially, if you order for a hamburger at a fast food restaurant, it is expected to be delivered within seconds or minutes, and you might want to wait about thirty minutes before the pizza is delivered to you. The expectations vary in context and provided that the time of delivery takes longer than is expected or "too long," you are likely to analyze the team or deliveryman and regard them as being lazy or slow.

Silence: this type of nonverbal communication involves using words or utterances to convey their meanings. Sometimes, we say an individual close to us is giving us the "silent treatment," that term describes when an individual is being silent and does not respond when he or she should. Behind the silence of the individual however, there are meanings to it. Silence is especially powerful because the individual that is being silent is refusing to communicate with you, which could indicate anger or other variants of emotion. Silence can be used to regulate the flow of conversations between people. Silence has several meanings, in similar ways that other types of nonverbal communication does.

Context plays a major role in determining the meaning of silence. It could be used to express discontent, anger or bitterness among others. An example of a situation where silence is used is during the silent protest that is carried out by students every year since 1996. This protest is carried out in order to get people to stand up for the rights of LGBTQ people. This movement believes that silence sends a louder message than any word they could think to use.

Paralanguage: paralanguage refers to the term used to describe vocal qualities which include volume, rhythm, the rate of speech, inflection, and pitch. Although nonverbal communication is used to describe communications made without speaking or writing, as seen in the types of communication already mentioned, this nonverbal communication, however, describes communication that involves being vocal (where a sound is produced). The way we say our words often express a great deal of meaning, even more than the actual words spoken do. An example of these is Sarcasm and Incongruence.

Some comedians, such as Stephen Wright make use of paralanguage in a large number of their comedies. The man talks using a completely monotone voice throughout his act and usually make use of statements such as "I'm getting really excited," while using the same monotone voice, along with a completely blank facial expression. The humor in his comedy cues in the Incongruence, i.e. his use of paralanguage and facial expression to contradict the message he is trying to pass verbally.

Whenever sarcasm is employed in a situation, paralanguage is intended to be in contrast with the verbal message the individual is trying to convey. Sarcasm can, however, backfire, especially when the people who the message is being directed at fails to pick up the paralinguistic cues that follow the message and instead focus primarily on the verbal message that is being passed.

Perhaps you are conversant with what is known as a pregnant pause, which is a silence that exists between verbal messages; the pause is, however, laced with meaning. This meaning may be difficult to understand or decipher, it is, however, present all the same. An example of this includes a coworker of yours, let's call him James returning from a sales meeting dumbstruck and with an expression like he's seen a ghost. You may ask him how the meeting went and he could reply saying 'well, ahh..." The pause speaks volume. It may indicate that something happened which you may not be aware of. It could be personal to James alone, or it could be more systemic.

Consider the powerful effect that the tone of voice used by an individual is bound to have on the meaning of a sentence. When the message is verbally spoken using a strong tone of voice, the listeners are apt to interpret it as enthusiasm and approval, when the same words are however used but with a hesitant tone of voice, the words may indicate disapproval and/or lack of interest. When you are asked "how are you?" and you are reply with a cold tone of voice might be interpreted as you not being fine, while a happy and bright tone of voice might be interpreted as you doing quite well. Using a somber and downcast tone would indicate that the individual is actually the opposite of fine.

If you think about it, the several ways by which we can communicate effectively without using verbal means is really astonishing.

Principles of Nonverbal Communication

There are five key principles you should have in mind when you are attempting to hone your skills in recognizing nonverbal cues and interpreting them, they include:

The age, gender, culture and geographic location are important.

Gestures are not universal. They mean different things in different regions. So, it will be wrong to generalize what one gesture means in one gesture to another. Culture and Family norms also influence the way and manner we react to nonverbal cues i.e. they are culture-specific.

Put things into context

Do not jump into conclusion. Put the individual, timing, the conversation, and other external influences into the context of the topic being discussed before you make your conclusion. A person might cross his or her arms, not because he or she is angry, such a person may only be cold.

Look for a combination of signals.

It is extremely difficult for the whole of our body to lie. People are able to hide their true intentions, however, irrespective of how long they are able to hide it, the real meaning often leaks through several channels. Paying attention to the body signals as a whole, from body language to tone of voice etc. will enable you to recognize the nonverbal cues and note when an individual lie.

Trust your Intuition

Intuition refers to the unconscious processing of information (in this context subtle nonverbal cues) that is manifested as physical feelings. Authenticity is cogent in identifying nonverbal cues since people identify inauthentic and insincere communication easily. The more aware you are of both the spoken and unspoken messages, the more heightened your instincts become.

Incongruence can suggest several things

When words and nonverbal cues are not in alignment, instincts come into play. Psychological discomforts could be an indication that you are being told lies, however, the feeling could mean other things. When an individual becomes more attuned to interpreting nonverbal signals and defines the ability, it leads to an increase in the individual to be more in tune with their instincts.

How to Improve Nonverbal Communication

Learn to manage stress

Stress affects your ability to communicate. Whenever you are stressed out, your ability to read becomes affected, making you more likely to misread other people, thereby sending confusing nonverbal signals, which is prone to result in knee-jerk patterns of behavior. Note, however, that emotions are contagious. If you are stressed and upset, it becomes more likely that you make others upset, thereby making the situation worse. So, if you are feeling overwhelmed by stress, it is essential that you take a time out. Calm yourself down before you enter into the conversation.

The fastest way by which you can manage stress is, however, by employing your senses, through a soothing movement that appeals to the senses.

Develop your Emotional Awareness

Before you can send and identify nonverbal signals, you need to be in touch with your emotions and how they affect you. Also, you should be able to identify the emotions of other people and what they truly feel behind the cues they are sending. When you are emotionally aware, you are able to:

Read other people accurately and be aware of the emotions they feel and the nonverbal messages they are sending.

Build trust in relationships by sending nonverbal cues that align with your verbal messages.

Respond to other people in ways that show that you understand and care for them.

Pay Attention to Nonverbal Signals

People are able to communicate information in several ways, therefore pay attention to those things like eye contact, body movements, posture etc., that are used to convey messages that are not put into words. When you pay close attention to the unspoken behaviors of other people, you will be able to improve on your ability to communicate nonverbally.

Look out for Incongruent Behaviors

Pay careful attention to people so that you will be aware of their words and if they do not match with their nonverbal behaviors. For example, when someone tells you they are happy while frowning. Research has proven that when words do not align with nonverbal cues, people are prone to ignore the verbal messages and instead focus on the nonverbal cues such as moods and emotions.

Concentrate on your Tone of Voice

Your tone of voice includes information which ranges from enthusiasm to anger to disinterest. Also, start noticing the effect your tone of voice has on the response of the people around you and try to use your tone in emphasizing the message you wish to communicate.

Use Good Eye Contact

Another nonverbal skill essential for you to possess is good eye contact. Failure of an individual to look others in the eye often seem like the individual is attempting to hide something. On the other hand, maintaining too much eye contact may seem intimidating or confrontational. Good eye contact does not necessarily mean that you have to stare unblinkingly into other people's eyes. How then, are you able to tell when eye contact is enough or not? Some communication experts recommend that eye contacts should last only about four to five seconds at intervals. Effective eye contact should also allow you and the other person feel natural and comfortable.

Ask Questions

If you are confused concerning the nonverbal cues of another person, you should ask questions. Repeating your interpretation of the cues, and then asking for clarification is permitted. Sometimes, when you ask questions concerning these cues, a great deal of clarity is placed on the subject.

Be aware that signals can be misread

For example, some people believe that when a handshake is firm, it is an indication of a strong personality, while weak handshakes indicate lack of fortitude. A mild handshake sometimes might indicate something other than the lack of fortitude, such as arthritis. Make sure to read the overall nonverbal cues and bot the single gesture.

Keep on Practicing

Some people seem to be able to use nonverbal communications effectively and correctly by interpreting the cues received from others. If you keep on practicing and attempting to effectively interpret nonverbal cues, with time, you get used to it.

Functions of Nonverbal Communication

Even though they do not involve the use of words, the importance and function of nonverbal cues in helping us communicate meanings more effectively include:

To duplicate verbal communication

When nonverbal cues can be recognized by most of the members of a particular cultural group, nonverbal communication can be used to duplicate verbal messages. Examples of these include shaking the head or nodding the head, as a duplicate for verbal messages of "yes" or "no."

Such include, replying a question asked with a verbal "yes" and then nodding your head. This action accomplishes the goal of duplicating the verbal message with a nonverbal message. The head nod is regarded as a "nearly universal indication of an accord, agreement, and understanding."

To replace verbal communication

When a question is asked and instead of you replying with a verbal "yes" and a head-nod such as in duplication, you may choose to only nod your head without the verbal message that accompanies it. When nonverbal cues replace verbal messages, nonverbal signals that would be easily recognized should be used such as a head-nod, a head-shake or a wave.

To complement verbal communication

When a friend tells you he or she received a promotion and a pay raise in recent times, there are a number of ways, both verbal and nonverbal to show your enthusiasm. Smiling and hugging your friend while exclaiming in joy is an example of ways in which nonverbal communication is used to complement verbal communication. Unlike nonverbal communication for duplicating and replacing, nonverbal communication for complementing cannot be used alone, it should always be accompanied by verbal messages.

To accent verbal communication

While nonverbal communication can be used to complement verbal communication, it can also be used to accent verbal communication by emphasizing particular aspects of the verbal message. For example, when you are extremely upset with someone, you say "I am very angry with you," however, to accent it nonverbally, you say "I am VERY angry with you" placing emphasis on the word "very," by poking the air with your fingers, raising your voice etc. in order to demonstrate the intensity of your anger.

To regulate verbal communication

With nonverbal communication, it is easier to enter, maintain and exit interactions with others. It is only on extremely rare occasions, if ever, that one person would approach the other and say to him "Let us start a conversation right now, alright, let us begin." It is much easier and convenient to make eye contact, move closer to the individual and face he or she directly using nonverbal behaviors that indicate the desire to interact. Also, when the conversation is about to end, it does not simply end by saying "Let us stop talking, I am done talking to you," except there is a breakdown in the process of communication. What we instead do is using nonverbal communication by looking at our watch and in the direction we wish to go. We could also become silent in order to indicate that an end is coming to the conversation. Although, verbal messages can be sent if there is a breakdown in the communication process.

To contradict verbal communication

In such a situation where you visit the office of your boss and you are asked about the new work assignment you have been given. You would probably feel obligated to respond to the question positively because it is your boss asking the question, even though you may not feel that way. However, the nonverbal cues you give may contradict the verbal message, thereby indicating to your boss that you do not enjoy the new work assigned to you. This example has the nonverbal communication contradict verbal communication and sending a mixed message to your bias.

Research, however, suggests that when verbal and nonverbal messages contradict one another, the receiver of the message is prone to place more value on the message perceived to be more accurate.

To mislead others

Nonverbal communications can be used to deceive, thereby mislead other people. If you are trying to detect deception, focusing on the nonverbal communication of the person is important. There could have been a time when someone asked your opinion of the new hairstyle they have, if you did not like it, you can verbally state that you did like the haircut and then provide nonverbal cues in order to further deceive the person about the way you really feel concerning the hairstyle. Also, when we are to determine if someone is trying to deceive or mislead us, we are apt to focus on the nonverbal values of the other person.

A study, however, suggests that when we try to detect deception in others through the nonverbal communications they make, we are able to detect 78% of lies and truths. However, other studies suggest that we are not as effective as we think we are at determining when other people are being deceitful; we are also only accurate about 45 to 70% of the time. When trying to detect deceit, it is usually made effective if both the verbal and nonverbal communication methods are carefully examined in order to prove their consistency (or lack of).

To indicate relational standing

If you take a few moments to observe the nonverbal communication that exists between people in public areas, you might be able to determine the relational standings from their nonverbal communication. For instance, you will find that romantic partners tend to stay close to one another and touch themselves frequently while acquaintances generally maintain greater distances than romantic partners and touch themselves less. Also, people who are of higher social status are apt to maintain more space during their interactions with others.

To demonstrate and maintain cultural norms

It is an established fact that some forms of nonverbal communication are universal, however, most of these nonverbal cues are culturally specific. For instance, in the culture of the United States, you will find that people are apt to place a high value on their personal space than in some other cultures and if someone accidentally touches you, he/she might apologize profusely for violating your personal space. The cultural norms of anxiety and fear as regards issues of crime and terrorism may cause people to be more sensitive and wary to others especially in public spaces. This is however in contrast with several Asian cultures where frequent touches go unnoticed in crowded public spaces because of the difference in the negotiation of space in both cultures.

To communicate emotions

It is in many ways possible to verbally express how we feel to other people, however, we use Nonverbal means more frequently. Conversely, we are prone to interpreting emotions by examining nonverbal communications. For example, an individual may be feeling sad and it would be easy to tell through the nonverbal communication he or she makes. The individual may not smile or may have his or her shoulder slumped and be less talkative.

A study suggests that using and interpreting nonverbal communication for emotional expression and eventually, satisfaction and relational attachment is important.

Understanding yourself and different personality types

Personality types refer to a system of categorizing people based on the tendencies they have to act and think in a particular manner. This system of categorization attempts to find the broadest and most important ways to differentiate people, and also, it tries to make sense of these differences by categorizing people into different meaningful groups.

The personality types described in this chapter were created by Isabel Briggs Myers and her mother, Katherine Briggs in the 1960s. Their theories depended on the ideas of a psychologist Carl Jung, whose works they extended into a complete framework for personality types.

The different personality type to which each individual belongs can be used to make generalizations concerning the individual. It also makes the job of analyzing the individual much easier, because it is in itself an analysis made of people, their behaviors and thought processes. Being able to categorize individuals into any of the 16 personality types described in this article is indeed a big step into being able to read people.

Four major dimensions were used to categorize people:

- Introversion vs. Extraversion (I/E)
- Sensing vs. iNtuitive (S/N)
- Thinking vs. Feeling (T/F)
- Judging vs. Perceiving (J/P)

Each of these dimensions was regarded as being a dichotomy and it was proposed that the sum of the four preferred styles by the individual is the personality type of the individual. People who share the same type of personality are bound to have several similarities in the way and manner in which they approach events and react to the stimuli in their lives, from the hobbies they choose to their types of humor and the type of work that suits them.

What do the dimensions' mean?

I/E. This dimension describes the way with which an individual manages his/her energy

Introversion (I): introverts tend to be thoughtful and reserved. They are energized by spending their time alone or with a small group.

Extraversion (E). Extraverts are outspoken and expressive. They are energized by spending time with people and inactive surroundings.

S/N. This dimension describes the way an individual processes information

Sensing (S). Sensors focus all their senses and are interested in the information they can perceive themselves either through sight, smell, touch, sound and so on. They are often regarded as being practical and they tend to learn hands-on.

iNtuitive (N): intuitive tend to focus more on an abstract level of thought and are interested in explanations, patterns, and theories. They are often regarded as being creative and they are more concerned with the future than the present.

T/F. This dimension describes the way people make decisions.

Thinking (T). Thinkers are prone to make decisions with their heads; they want to find the most logical and reasonable choice.

Feeling (F). Feelers are prone to making decisions with their hearts; they want to know how a decision will influence the people and also if it will fit in with their values.

J/P. This dimension describes the way people approach structures and issues in their lives.

Judging (J). Judgers tend to appreciate structure and order; they like to make plans and follow it, and they dislike making changes at the last minute.

Perceiving (P). Perceivers tend to appreciate spontaneity and flexibility; they like to leave things open so that they will be able to make changes if they desire.

INFP

An acronym for Introverted, iNtuitive, Feeling and Perceiving.

INFP describes a person who is energized by spending time alone, focuses on ideas, concepts, theories, rather than facts and details, makes decisions based on their values and feelings and is spontaneous and flexible rather than planned and organized. They are sometimes referred to as healer personalities because of their gentle compassion and sympathetic idealism.

INFPs are imaginative idealists and they work according to their beliefs and values. They tend to see the potential for a better future and they are engaged in the search for truth and meaning with their own flair.

INFPs are sensitive, caring, individualistic and nonjudgmental. They believe that each person has to find his/her own path and they enjoy taking their time to explore their values and ideas, enjoining others to do the same. They are creative and artistic.

INFPs are usually offbeat and unconventional without any desire to conform. Individuals with INFP would rather be outcasts than fit in with the crowd.

INFPs do not judge people, they are flexible, supportive and accommodating. They hate when their rights are violated by others and they hate being steamrolled by people. They are open and they support the exchange of ideas.

INTI

An acronym for Introverted, iNtuitive, Thinking, Judging.

INTI describes a person who is energized by spending time alone, focuses on ideas, concepts, and theories instead of facts and details, makes decisions based on reason and logic and prefers to be planned and organized as opposed to flexible and spontaneous. They are sometimes referred to as mastermind personalities as a result of their logical and strategic way of thinking.

INTIs are analytical problem solvers and they are usually eager to improve processes and systems with their innovative ideas. They tend to see opportunities for improvement, be it in their work, at their home or in themselves.

INTIs are intellectuals. They enjoy complex problem-solving and logical reasoning. They go through life by first analyzing the theory behind the things they see. They tend to focus inward, in their study of the world. They are not particularly comfortable with the unpredictable nature known to people and their emotions. They are independent and selective with the people they associate with, preferring people they regard as intellectually stimulating.

They are perceptive about strategy, processes, and systems, and they desire to understand them. They are able to foresee logical outcomes. They are perfectionists with extremely high standards. They strive to increase their competence.

INFJ

An acronym for Introverted, iNtuitive, Feeling, Judging.

INFJ describes a person who is energized by spending time alone, concentrates on ideas and concepts and makes decisions based on their feelings and values and prefers to be organized and planned. They are often referred to as Counselor personalities.

INFJs are creative nurturers and they have a strong sense of integrity and a drive to help others achieve their potential. They are creative and loyal with the ability to intuit the emotions and motivations of others. They are insightful and trusts in their ability to read people. They are sensitive, reserved and they are selective as regards sharing their personal thoughts and feelings.

INFJs have a deeply considered set of personal values. They are idealists and imaginative. They are easily discouraged by the harsh circumstances of the present, and yet feel the intrinsic drive to make situations better.

INFJs desire a meaningful life and also deep connections with others and they appreciate emotional intimacy with a select few.

INTP

An acronym for Introverted, iNtuitive, Thinking, Perceiving.

INTP describes a person who prefers to spend time alone, concentrates on ideas and concepts, makes decisions based on reason and logic and are spontaneous and flexible. They are often referred to as Architect personalities because of their Intuitive understanding of complex systems.

INTPs are philosophical innovators and are fascinated by logical analysis, design, and systems. They desire the understanding of the themes that unify life in their complexity. They are often engaged in the search for the universal law behind the physical. They are detached, analytical observers, who spend a lot of time on their thoughts, exploring concepts, making connections and trying to understand.

INTPs are passionate about innovation, analysis, and reason. They have complicated and active minds and they strive to arrive at ingenious solutions to interesting problems.

INTPs are nontraditional and are apt to not follow the crowd as they like to find things out for themselves.

ENTJ

An acronym for Extraverted, iNtuitive, Thinking, Judging.

ENTJ describes a person who is energized by spending time with others, focuses on ideas and concepts, makes decisions based on reason and logic and are organized and planned. They are sometimes regarded as Commander personalities because of their desire to lead.

ENTJs are strategic leaders, motivated to organize change; they detect inefficiencies easily and conceptualize nee solutions. They enjoy making long-range plans in accomplishing their vision. They are articulate, quick-witted and reason logically.

ENTJs are analytical and objective with the desire to bring order to their world. They are assertive and enjoys taking charge.

ENTJs are usually motivated by success and hard work; they are ambitious with interest in acquiring power and influence. They consider decision-making to be a vocation and they like to call the shots.

ENTJs are blunt and decisive; they can be brusque and critical and they are driven to get things done. They are friendly, outgoing, but might not attend to the feelings of others.

ENTP

An acronym for Extraverted, iNtuitive, Thinking, Perceiving.

ENTP describes a person who is energized by spending time with others, focuses on ideas and theories, makes decisions based on reason and logic and prefers to be spontaneous and flexible. They are often regarded as Visionary personalities because of their drive for new, innovative ideas

ENTPs are inspired by innovators and are motivated to solving intellectually challenging problems. They are furious and clever and desires to understand people, processes and systems around them. They are open-minded and unconventional. They desire to analyze, understand and influence others.

ENTPs likes toying with ideas and bantering with people. They are quick-witted with an excellent command of a language. They often like poking fun at their habits and eccentricities. They enjoy challenging others, but they are also happy to live and let live. They are rarely judgmental. They have little patience for slow people.

They are confident in their abilities, and they often rely on their ingenuity to deal with the world without making preparations. They question and ignore norms and are innovative.

ENFJ

An acronym for Extraverted, iNtuitive, Feeling, Judging.

ENFJ describes a person who is energized by spending time with others, focuses on ideas and theories, makes decisions based on feelings and values and are planned and organized. They are sometimes called Teacher personalities because of their desire to help others grow.

ENFJs are idealist organizers, driven to implement their vision for humanity. They are often catalysts for human growth and are able to see potential in others. They are charismatic in persuading others to their own ideas. They are passionate about the possibilities for people and concentrate on their values and vision.

ENFJs are energetic and driven. They are attuned to the needs of others and they know when people suffer, however, they are optimistic and intuitively seek opportunity for improvement. They are ambitious and feel personally responsible for improving the world.

ENFJs are altruistic and empathetic, they are humanitarian in nature and they believe in cooperation. They are very sensitive and they expect the best from everyone. They work hard to maintain their relationships

ENFP

An acronym for Extraverted, iNtuitive, Feeling, Perceiving.

ENFPs describes a person who is energized by spending time with others, concentrates on ideas and concepts, makes decisions based on feelings and values and are spontaneous and flexible. They are sometimes regarded as Champion personalities because of their drive to help others achieve their dreams.

ENFPs are people-centered and they focus on possibilities and are enthusiastic about new ideas, people and activities. They are warm, passionate and energetic. They are witty, humorous and masters of language. They are agile, expressive communicators and are often artistic

They are curious about others and are often engaged with discovering the deeper meaning to people and ideas. They desire authenticity and emotional intensity. They are easily bored by the mundane, details and repetitions. They place great value on self-expression and personal value. They are nonjudgmental, warm and dislikes the harsh reality.

ISFJ

An acronym for Introverted, Sensing, Feeling, Judging.

ISFJ describes a person who is energized by spending time alone, focuses on facts and details, makes decisions based on feelings and values and are planned and organized. They are sometimes regarded as Protector personalities because they like keeping people safe and well-cared for.

iSFJs are industrious caretakers they are loyal to traditions, practical, compassionate and caring. They are conventional and grounded and enjoys contributing to the structures of society. They are committed and steady with a deep sense of responsibility to others. They are conscientious, methodical and unrelenting.

ISFJs are humble, unassuming, compassionate, loyal and hardworking. They value relationships, strive to maintain harmony and cooperate with others. They are stable and desire longevity in their relationships. They are involved in social groups, yet they do not want the spotlight.

ISFP

An acronym for Introverted, Sensing, Feeling, Perceiving.

ISFP describes a person who is energized by spending time alone, focuses on facts and details, makes decisions based on feelings and values and are spontaneous and flexible. They are often referred to as Composer personalities because of their innate sensibility for producing aesthetically pleasing experiences.

ISFPs are gentle caretakers and they tend to live in the moment, enjoying their surroundings with low-key, cheerful enthusiasm. They are quiet, unassuming and may be hard to know. They are warm, friendly and eager to share life's experiences. They have a strong aesthetic sense and seek out beauty around them. They have a natural talent for art and they excel at manipulating the arts.

ISFPs are loyal, tolerant and nonjudgmental, they are accepting and supportive. They are modest and may underestimate themselves. They prefer to be supporting and are rarely ambitious.

ISTJ

An acronym for Introverted, Sensing, Thinking, Judging.

ISTJ describes a person who is energized by spending time alone, focuses on facts and details, makes decisions based on reason and logic and are organized and planned. They are often referred to as Inspector personalities because they focus on details and have an interest in doing things properly.

ISTJs are responsible organizers motivated to create and enforce order within systems. They are neat, reliable and dutiful. They tend to uphold tradition and follow procedures. They are steady, productive contributors and are rarely isolated. They know where they belong in life and wants to understand how to participate in the system.

ISTJs desires to know the rules of the game. They value predictability more than imagination. They use their past experience as a guide and are most comfortable in familiar environments. They trust the established method and value dedicated practice. They are hardworking and unrelenting. They are loyal, meticulous, diligent and attentive.

ISTP

An acronym for Introverted, Sensing, Thinking, Perceiving.

ISTP describes a person who is energized by spending time alone, focuses on facts and details, make decisions based on reason and logic and prefers spontaneity and flexibility. They are sometimes regarded as Craftsman personalities because of their innate mechanical ability and facility with tools.

ISTPs are observant artisans who understand mechanics. They approach their surroundings with a flexible logic. They are independent and adaptable and interactive in a self-directed, spontaneous manner. They are attentive to details and responsive to the world. They are good in emergencies, reserved, yet not withdrawn. They take action and they appreciate physical and sensory experiences.

They tend to study how things work and achieve mastery in operating machines, equipment and instruments. They get bored by theory easily. They tend to be detached and prefer mechanical activities to human emotions. They are independent and reserved, tolerant and nonjudgmental. They are private and action takers.

ESFJ

An acronym for Extraverted, Sensing, Feeling, Judging.

ESFJ describes a person who is energized by spending time with others, focuses on details and facts, makes decisions based on values and feelings and are planned and organized. They are often referred to as Provider personalities because they like to care for others in practical ways.

ESFJs are often playing host or hostess, and they can play an organizer without hesitation. They engage in community duties and work hard to maintain social order. They are interested in others and prefer gossip as a pastime. They are loyal and value tradition. They are empathetic and generous.

ESFJs have a clear moral code guiding their behaviors and expectations. They are strongly opinionated about how others behave and the proper way to do things. They may think in black and white. They may be judgmental but have the best intentions. They are attuned to their emotional environment and the feelings of others. They are eager to please and provide and they seek cooperation and harmony.

ESFP

An acronym for Extraverted, Sensing, Feeling, Perceiving.

ESFP describes a person who is energized by spending time with others, focuses on details and facts, makes decisions based on values and feelings and prefer spontaneity and flexibility. They are regarded as Performer personalities because of their playful, energetic nature.

ESFPs are vivacious entertainers capable of charming and engaging the people around them. They are spontaneous, energetic, fun-loving and find pleasure in things around them. They are warm, talkative and contagious. They like being the center of attention. They like to have a good time.

ESFPs likes been busy. They are down-to-earth, observant and responsive in offering assistance. They are friendly and likable and reluctant to be serious. They often choose fabrics and decorations to surround themselves carefully. They may take the lead in creating an active diversion.

ESTJ

An acronym for Extraverted, Sensing, Thinking, Judging.

ESTJ describes a person who is energized by spending time with others, focuses on details and facts, make decisions based on reason and logic and prefers planning and organization. They are regarded as Supervisor personalities because they tend to take charge, making sure things are done properly.

ESTJs command a situation with the sense of how things should go. They are task-oriented and often put work before play. They are confident and tough-minded and appears to be in control almost always. They appreciate structure and establish ground rules. They respect and seek out the hierarchy.

ESTJs are hardworking traditionalists, conscientious and rule-abiding. They value predictability and organization. They often take the initiative to create guidelines and processes in order to ensure that everyone knows what is expected of them.

ESTP

An acronym for Extraverted, Sensing, Thinking, Perceiving.

ESTPs describes a person who is energized by spending time with others, focuses on details and facts, make decisions based on reason and logic and prefers spontaneity and flexibility. They are often regarded as Dynamo personalities because of their active and high-energy approach to life.

ESTPs are energetic and they often chat, joke and flirt. They like keeping people on their toes with their fun. They are gregarious with people. Their interest in people does not last long. They are comfortable in their physical environment and likes action and activity. They are the most coordinated of all the types. They are adrenaline junkies.

ESTPs are energetic thrill seekers. They bring dynamic energy to their interactions with people and the world. They assess situations quickly and respond immediately. They are active and playful, the life of the party and also have a good sense of humor. They are very social.

ESTPs enjoy risky or dangerous activities. They are excellent in emergencies.

The Limbic Brain

There are certain times when we need to look beyond ourselves, beyond our power of observation and focus instead on the neurological processes that go on in the individual. Virtually all individuals are similar yet different in the composition of their physiology, it is for this reason that it may be easier for some people to understand emotions, and interpret certain cues better than other people. If you, however, desire to analyze people, you need to be conversant with the processes that go on inside of you and human beings in general in order to arrive at better conclusions and decisions concerning observed behaviors. One major part of the body to study so as to achieve this is the human brain.

The human brain happens to be one of the most wonderful structures present in the human body. Although, it is one of the most studied parts, there are still several functions it performs that are yet to be discovered. It is, however, known that there are several systems that exist within the brain and they have specialized roles which they perform in order to make our body work. One of the most important systems currently known to man is the Limbic System.

The Limbic system as it is called today was conceptualized in 1949 by a physiologist called MacLean, and it was an extension of the first conceptualization of the system initiated in 1939 by Papez, and it gave it the current name.

The Limbic Brain is also regarded as the emotional brain and it is made up of several brain structures which are all interconnected. These structures exist on both sides of the thalamus, right under the cerebrum. They also make it difficult to determine precisely the structures that make up the Limbic system and the function of each structure. Studies, however, suggests that there are essentially six different structures that make up the Limbic Brain and they include the hypothalamus, the hippocampus, the amygdala, and several other nearby areas.

The Limbic system is considered to be primarily responsible for our emotional life, and it deals with the formation of memories., amongst others.

The Components of the Limbic Brain

The six major components of the Limbic Brain have been mentioned above and they include:

Amygdala

Basal ganglia

Cingulate gyrus

Hippocampus

Hypothalamus and

Thalamus.

Amygdala

Location: The Amygdala is located deep within the temporal lobe, adjacent to the hippocampus and medial to the hypothalamus.

The Amygdala is a mass of nuclei (mass of cells) with the shape of an almond that is located deep within the temporal lobes of the brain. There are two amygdalae and each one is situated in the two brain hemispheres. The amygdala is a Limbic system structure that is involved in several of our emotions, emotional behaviors, and motivation, especially the ones that are related to survival. It is involved in processing emotions such as fear, pleasure, and anger, and it is responsible for determining the memories that are stored and the part of the brain they are stored in.

Anatomy

The amygdala is made up of a large cluster of about 13 nuclei, which are subdivided into smaller units. The largest of these subdivisions is the basolateral complex which is made up of the accessory nucleus, basolateral nucleus, and lateral nucleus. This subdivision is connected with the thalamus cerebral cortex and the hippocampus. When information is transmitted from the olfactory system, it is received by two separate groups of amygdaloid nuclei: the medial nucleus and the cortical nuclei. The nuclei of the amygdala are also connected with the brainstem and the hypothalamus.

The brainstem helps to transmit information between the cerebrum and the spinal cord while the hypothalamus is involved in emotional responses and it helps to regulate the endocrine system.

The connections made to these areas of the brain permits the amygdaloid nuclei to process information from sensory areas (which include the cortex and the thalamus) and the areas that are associated with autonomic function and behavior (which include th3 brainstem and the hypothalamus).

Sensory Information

The fibers that carry inputs to the amygdala are usually combined with fibers that carry outputs from the amygdala. The amygdala receives inputs from all the senses of the body as well as the visceral inputs. The amygdala is an important factor for emotional learning, which makes the visceral inputs a major input source.

Effects of the Amygdala

The main purpose the amygdala serves is emotional and social processing. The amygdala receives several connections from the hippocampus which is in charge of storing and retrieving explicit memories and then processing the context of a situation. It is believed that these connections of the hippocampus with the amygdala is responsible for eliciting strong emotions which might be triggered by certain memories.

The amygdala plays an important role in the coordination of our responses (be it autonomic, behavioral and endocrine) to the environmental stimuli. It allows us to attend to the stimuli from the environment in a coordinated manner.

It plays an extremely vital role in both behavioral and reflexive responses that are necessary for survival during stress.

The amygdala is an important part of fear conditioning and the fight or flight response. During fight and flight response, impulses from the central nervous system are transmitted to the central gray matter so as to initiate a message that will bring an end to the dangerous activity. The impulses to the lateral hypothalamus help to increase blood pressure and the rate of heartbeat in order to get the body prepared for a quick response.

When impulses are transmitted to the facial nerves, they generate facial expressions that indicate emotions like anger, fear etc.

Several studies have shown that the amygdala plays a vital role in processing emotions especially fear conditioning, one of these studies was conducted by Paul Bucy and Heinrich Oliver in 1939. This study involves removing the temporal lobes on both sides (including the amygdala and hippocampus) in monkeys. The emotional behavior of the monkey was then observed. The result of this alteration was that the monkey became tame and its sexual activity increased.

Studies have also shown that emotional stimuli, such as emotional expressions are capable of activating the amygdala. This is evident in a rare disorder called Urbach-Wiethe disease. This disease involves isolated lesions of the amygdala. Patients suffering from this disorder are unable to differentiate between emotions in facial expressions.

When people become affected by psychological disorders such as PTSD, depression, autism, schizophrenia, phobia and much more, changes occur to the amygdala in them. This might, however, be due to the fact that the amygdala plays an important role in conditioning fear, and these disorders are related to fear and anxiety in some way.

When a threat is perceived, a part of the stimulus proceeds directly to the amygdala. If the stimulus is considered to be a fight-or-flight situation by the amygdala as a result of last experiences kept in the hippocampus, the HPA (hypothalamic-pituitary-adrenal) axis is triggered. If the stimulus is not considered as threatening, it acts according to the information received from the neocortex (or rational brain). This describes amygdala hijack which is essentially a situation whereby the emotional response elicited is not in accordance with the stimulus perceived. It involves the onset of a strong emotional reaction which is realized at a later time to be inappropriate.

Fear Conditioning

Emotion linked to perceptual experience is regarded as Fear conditioning. A large number of the things we know about the amygdala and the role it plays in emotional learning and memory is a result of fear conditioning which was conducted majorly with animals. It is similar to classical conditioning performed by Ivan Pavlov.

Disorders of the Amygdala

When the amygdala is hyperactive or one amygdala is smaller than the other one, the result is often associated with fear and anxiety disorders. Anxiety is a psychological response to events or stimuli that are perceived as dangerous, while Fear is both the emotional and physical response to danger. Anxiety can result in panic attacks when the amygdala transmits signals that a person is in danger when there is no real threat. Anxiety disorders related to amygdala can cause such disorders as Post-Traumatic Stress Disorder (PTSD), Borderline Personality Disorder (BPD), Obsessive-Compulsive Disorder and Social Anxiety Disorder.

Basal Ganglia

Location: The basal ganglia are situated deep within the cerebral hemispheres of the brain., they are found on both sides of the thalamus, above and outside the Limbic system, within the temporal lobes and below the cingulate gyrus.

The basal ganglia are a group of neurons (or nuclei) that consists of the corpus striatum (which is the major group of basal ganglia nuclei) and related nuclei. This component of the Limbic system is involved majorly in processing information related to movements. They are also involved in processing information that is related to emotions, cognitive functions, and motivations. The basal ganglia dysfunction is related to a number of disorders that affect movement which includes Huntington disease, Parkinson's disease and Uncontrolled or Slow movement (dystonia).

The Corpus Stratium

The largest group of the nuclei of basal ganglia is the corpus stratium ("striped body"), which is made of the caudate nucleus ("tail-like nucleus"), the global pallidus ("pale globe"), the putamen ("nutshell") and the nucleus accumbens ("leaning nucleus"). The caudate nucleus, putamen and nucleus accumbens are considered to be input nuclei, while global pallidus is considered to be output nuclei. The corpus stratium makes use of and stores the neurotransmitter dopamine. It is also associated with the reward circuit of the brain.

Caudate Nuclei

Caudate nuclei are c-shaped paired nuclei (with one located in each hemisphere) situated primarily in the frontal lobe region of the brain. These nuclei have a head region that curves and extends thereby resulting in an elongated body that goes on to taper at its tail. The caudate begins behind the frontal lobe and then curves back towards the occipital lobe and its tail end in the temporal lobe of the amygdala. It transmits messages to the frontal lobe and seems to be in charge of informing us when something is not right, thereby prodding us to do something about it. Such as "Lock the door!" Wash your hands!" etc. These examples are suggestive of situations that may involve several disorders such as Obsessive-compulsive disorders, Attention-Deficit disorder, the depression aspects of schizophrenia, and lethargy. Underactive caudate nucleus results in the onset of the aforementioned disorders.

The caudate nucleus is involved in motor processing, as well as planning. It is also involved in memory storage (both unconscious memory and long-term memory), inhibitory control, decision making, planning, associative and procedural learning.

Putamen

The putamen is a largely rounded nucleus (with one being in each hemisphere) located in the forebrain. They lie under and behind the front of the caudate nucleus. Along with the caudal nucleus, the putamen forms the dorsal stratium. This nucleus is connected to the caudate nucleus at the head region. It is also involved in both voluntary and involuntary motor control. The putamen seems to be involved in coordinating automatic behaviors which include driving a car, riding a bike or working in an assembly line. The problems associated with the putamen may be responsible for the symptoms of Tourette's syndrome.

Nucleus Accumbens

These paired nuclei (with one being in each hemisphere) are situated between the caudate nucleus and putamen. The nucleus accumbens along with the olfactory tubercle (which is the sensory processing center in the olfactory cortex) form the central region of the stratium. The nucleus accumbens receives signals from the prefrontal cortex through the ventral tegmental area and then transmit other signals back there through the global pallidus.

The signal inputs make use of dopamine and the many drugs are recognized as being able to increase the messages to the nucleus accumbens largely.

Global Pallidus

These paired nuclei (with one located in each hemisphere) are situated near the putamen and caudate nucleus. These nuclei are divided into two segments; external and internal segments and they act as one of the primary output nuclei of the basal ganglia. The global pallidus receives inputs from both the caudate nucleus and the putamen and then provide outputs to the substantia nigra. The internal segments of this nuclei transmit the majority of the output to the thalamus through the neurotransmitter Gamma-AminoButyric Acid (GABA). The effect of GABA on motor functions include inhibitions

The external segments of the global pallidus however, are intrinsic nuclei and they transmit information to other nuclei of the basal ganglia and the internal segments of the global pallidus. The global pallidus is involved in regulating voluntary movement.

Other nuclei of the basal ganglia:

Substantia nigra

This nucleus is a large mass and it is located in the upper parts of the midbrain. It is also a component of the brainstem. The substantia nigra is made up of the pars compacta and the pars reticulata. The pars reticulata segments form one of the primary inhibitory outputs of the basal ganglia and it aids in regulating eye movements. The pars compacta segment is made up of intrinsic nuclei that transmit information between both input and output sources. This segment is primarily involved in motor control and coordination.

The pars compacta contain pigmented nerve cells that produce dopamine. The neurons of the substantia nigra are connected with the dorsal stratium (caudate nucleus and putamen) and thereby provide the stratium with this dopamine. The substantia nigra also serves several functions ranging from controlling voluntary movements to learning, regulating moods and activities related brain's reward circuit.

Subthalamic nucleus

These nuclei are small-paired and they are a component of the diencephalon which is found beneath the thalamus. These nuclei receive excitatory inputs from the cerebral cortex and their connections to globus pallidus and the substantia nigra are excitatory. Subthalamic nuclei involve both input and output connections to the substantia nigra, putamen and caudate nucleus. The Subthalamic nucleus also plays a primary role in voluntary and involuntary movement and it is involved in limbic functions and associative learning.

Subthalamic nuclei have connections with the limbic system through their connections with nucleus accumbens and cingulate gyrus.

Functions of the Basal Ganglia

The basal ganglia and the nuclei associated with it are regarded as one of three types of nuclei

- Input nuclei receive signals from several sources in the brain.
- Output nuclei transmit signals from the basal ganglia to the thalamus.
- Intrinsic nuclei transmit nerve signals and information between the input nuclei and the output nuclei.

The basal ganglia receive information from the thalamus and cerebral cortex through the input nuclei. After processing the information, it is transmitted to the intrinsic nuclei which then send it to the output nuclei, from where the information is then passed to the cerebral cortex.

Disorder of Basal Ganglia

The dysfunction of the structures of basal ganglia often results in various movement disorder examples of which include Parkinson's disease, Dystonia, Huntington's disease, Tourette Syndrome and Multiple System Atrophy. These disorders are often as a result of the damage caused to the deep brain structures of the basal ganglia. The damage could be as a result of carbon monoxide poisoning, head injury, drug overdose, liver disease, heavy metal poisoning etc.

People who experience basal ganglia dysfunction are apt to exhibit difficulty in walking with slow or uncontrolled movements. They may also experience tremors, muscle spasms, increased muscle tone and problems controlling speech.

Cingulate Gyrus

Location: the cingulate gyrus is directionally superior to the corpus callosum. It is situated between the sulcus of the corpus callosum and the cingulate sulcus (groove or indentation).

A gyrus is regarded as a fold or "bulge" that exists in the brain. The cingulate gyrus is the curved fold in the brain that covers the corpus callosum. It is the component of the Limbic system that is associated with processing emotions and regulating behaviors. It is also involved in regulating autonomic motor function. The cingulate gyrus is divided into two segments: the anterior cingulate gyrus and the posterior cingulate gyrus. When damage is caused to the cingulate gyrus, it often results in disorders in important areas of the body which includes cognition, emotion, and behavior, therefore, it is involved in disorders such as

Alzheimer's disease, addiction, schizophrenia, depression, bipolar disorder and a host of others.

Anatomy

The cingulate gyrus begins beneath the rostrum of the corpus callosum and it runs through the width of the lamia terminalis to the anterior commissure curves that surround the front of the genu of corpus callosum, it travels further along the superior surface of the body before it terminates at a narrow isthmus which lies behind the splenium.

Effects of the Cingulate gyrus

The cingulate gyrus performs the following functions:

- It coordinates sensory input with emotions
- It aids communication
- It is involved with emotional responses to pain
- It is involved in language expression
- It aids decision making
- It aids maternal bonding

The Anterior Cingulate Gyrus

The anterior cingulate gyrus is associated with the performance of a number of functions which includes the processing and vocalization of emotions. This component is connected with the areas in the frontal lobes that is associated with speech and vocalization including the Broca's area, which is involved in controlling motor functions for the production of speech.

The anterior cingulate gyrus is associated with the development of emotional bond and attachment especially between the mother and her child. This bond comes into existence when frequent vocalization occurs between the mother and the infant. The anterior cingulate gyrus is also connected to the amygdala which is the brain structure that is involved with processing emotions and relating them to specific events, thereby enhancing the bonding process between the mother and her child.

The anterior cingulate gyrus works together with the amygdala in order to create fear conditioning and memory associated with the sensory information received from the thalamus. Another Limbic system, the hippocampus, is also related to the anterior cingulate gyrus, thereby playing a major role in the formation of memories and storage.

The anterior cingulate gyrus often collaborates with the hypothalamus in order to allow certain physiological controls which include regulating the release of endocrine hormones and also, the autonomic functions of the peripheral nervous system. These changes, however, occur when we experience emotions such as anger, excitement or fear. Some other functions include the regulation of heart rate, the regulation of blood pressure and the regulation of respiratory rate.

The anterior cingulate gyrus also aids in the process of making decisions. This is achieved when it detects errors and monitors negative results. This function of the cingulate gyrus helps us to plan our actions and responses in appropriate manners.

The Posterior Cingulate Gyrus

The posterior cingulate gyrus plays a vital role in spatial memory, which refers to the ability to process information that deals with the spatial orientation of the objects in an environment. The connections between the temporal lobes and parietal lobes enable the posterior cingulate gyrus to impact functions that are related to movement, spatial orientation, and navigation.

The connections between the posterior cingulate gyrus and the midbrain and spinal cord give the posterior cingulate gyrus enough room to transmit/relay signals between the brain and the spinal cord.

The dysfunction of Cingulate Gyrus

There are some emotional and behavioral disorders that are related to the cingulate gyrus and they include depression, obsessive-compulsive disorders, and anxiety disorders among others. The cingulate gyrus dysfunction has, however, been linked to autism, schizophrenia, anxiety disorders, attention-deficit disorder, etc.

The individuals that are associated with cingulate gyrus that do not function properly are prone to have problems with communicating and dealing with situations that changes constantly. Under these conditions, these individuals become easily frustrated or angry and also they have emotional and violent outbursts.

In physiological terms, individuals may experience chronic pain or display behaviors that are addictive such as drug or alcohol abuse and eating disorders.

Hippocampus

Location: The hippocampus is situated above each ear and about an inch-and-a-half in your head, in the inner folds of the lower middle section of the brain, otherwise known as the temporal lobe.

The hippocampus is a small, curved formation in the brain and it plays a major role in the limbic system. The hippocampus is associated with the formation of new memories and also with learning and emotions. This part of the brain is lateralized and symmetrical, thereby resulting in two hippocampi.

The hippocampus is associated with feelings and reactions. It is also a site for generating new nerve cells.

How the Hippocampus Affects Memory?

The hippocampus plays a major role in the process of formation, organization, and storage of new memories, and also in connecting specific emotions and sensations to these memories. Do you ever notice the way a particular scent or sound trigger a particular memory? That is one of the functions of the hippocampus in the connection.

Studies have shown that different subregions of the hippocampus play major roles in different types of memory. An example of this is the rear part of the hippocampus which is involved in processing spatial memories.

The hippocampus also plays a major role in consolidating memories during sleep. Research, however, shows that a higher amount of hippocampal activities that occurs during sleep follow some form of training or learning experience which then leads to better memory of the training or learning material the following day.

However, this is not an indication of the memories being stored in the hippocampus for the long term. It is instead believed that the hippocampus helps to transport the information -after taking them in, registering them and temporarily storing them- to long term memory. This process, however, requires sleep.

Functions

Memory

Historically, Brenda Milner and William Scoville were the first people to describe the link that exists between the hippocampus and the formation of long-term memory during their report of what happened to an epileptic patient who went through surgery on the organ that was purported to help him remove his seizures. The patient suffered severe amnesia after the surgical procedure and was unable to form new memories of events that had happened to him such as when or where a particular situation occurred (which is regarded as episodic memory). The only memories the patient could retain were the ones from several years prior to the surgical procedure, as far back as his childhood.

It is generally agreed by experts that the hippocampus has its own role to play in the detection of new stimuli, occurrences and surroundings and also in the formation of new memories. Some experts also believe that the hippocampus is involved in declarative memory, which is a memory that can be communicated verbally, example include facts and figures.

Behavioral Inhibition

Certain experiments involving animals have investigated the impact of hippocampal damage and the results suggest that damage to the hippocampus causes the individual to be hyperactive, and also that the ability to inhibit certain behaviors and responses that have been learned at a particular point in time is affected. Examples of this include restlessness, insomnia and so on.

Spatial Navigation and Spatial Memory

Neuroscientist John O'Keefe and Psychology Professor Lynn Nadel studied the contribution of the hippocampus to the formation of memory and learning behaviors in the 1960s and 1970s. The Neuroscientist and Professor wrote a book together in 1978 with the title "The Hippocampus as a Cognitive Map." The book describes the role of the hippocampus in the process of learning and storing information. Spatial relationships are essentially the routes and pathways used for memories. These routes and pathways are stored in the hippocampus.

Damages to the Hippocampus

If a part of the hippocampi or both parts is damaged or hurt either in an accident or by illnesses, the individual is prone to experiencing loss of memory and also to lose the ability to make new long-term memories. They may not be able to remember things that occur a short while before the hippocampus(i) was damaged, but they may be able to retrieve information that has been in storage for a long while because the long-term memories have been stored in a completely different part of the brain as soon as they become long term. These damages have also been linked to conditions such as Post-Traumatic Stress Disorder (PTSD) or Schizophrenia.

The diseases associated with this component of the Limbic system include Alzheimer's disease, epilepsy, Cushing's disease, depression and stress amongst others.

Hypothalamus

Location: The hypothalamus is situated beneath the thalamus and above the brain stem.

The hypothalamus is a small and vital component in the center of the brain. It plays a vital role in the production of hormones and in stimulating the important processes in the body.

Hormones of the Hypothalamus

In order to maintain homeostasis in the body, it is the duty of the hypothalamus to create or control the several hormones present in the body. The hypothalamus works with the pituitary gland which creates and transmits other vital hormones around the body, and together they control several of the hormone-producing glands of the body (endocrine system).

The hormones secreted by the hypothalamus include:

- antidiuretic hormone: this hormone increases the amount of water that the kidneys absorb into the blood.
- corticotropin-releasing hormone: this hormone helps to regulate immune response and metabolism by working with the adrenal and pituitary gland in the release of certain steroids.
- gonadotropin-releasing hormone: this hormone directs the pituitary gland to release more hormones in order to ensure the continuous function of the sexual organs.
- oxytocin: this hormone is involved in several processes which include regulating sleep cycles, moderating body temperature and release of a mother's breast milk.
- prolactin-controlling hormones: this hormone instructs the pituitary gland to either begin or stop the production of breast milk in lactating mothers.
- thyrotropin-releasing hormone: this hormone activates the thyroid, which is involved in releasing hormones that regulate energy levels, metabolism, and developmental growth.

The hypothalamus is also directly involved in influencing the growth of hormones. They instruct the pituitary gland to either increase or decrease the presence of these growth hormones in the body in order to provide the hormones essential for the growth of children and even developed adults.

Functions

The hypothalamus is essential for living as it plays a vital role. It directs certain metabolic processes and other activities associated with the autonomic nervous system. This component of the limbic brain synthesizes and secrete hypothalmic releasing hormones which control and regulates the secretion of pituitary hormones. The following include the functions performed by the hypothalamus. It;

- Regulates body temperature
- Controls sexual behavior and reproduction
- Controls the intake of food and water, hunger and thirst, appetite and weight control.
- Mediate emotional responses
- Controls the daily cycles of the physiological state and behavior, identified as circadian rhythm.
- Connects the endocrine and nervous system in a bid to achieve homeostasis.

Thalamus

Location: The thalamus is situated at the center of the brain, between the midbrain and the cerebral cortex.

Thalamus performs several functions in the body such as being an important relay and integrative station for passing sensory signals and motor information to the areas of the cerebral cortex, the hypothalamus, the brainstem, and the basal ganglia. It also helps to regulate sleep, alertness, and consciousness, anger and aggression etc.

Functions

The thalamus is composed of several complicated collections of nerve cells which are interconnected and placed in the brain.

During sleep, the thalamus reduces the transmission of information to the sensory-motor cortex through GABA-mediated inhibition.

For every sensory signal present (except for the olfactory system), there are thalamic nuclei, and they receive these sensory signals and transmit them to the cortical areas they are associated with.

The lateral geniculate system of the thalamus is associated with the visual system. This nucleus receives sensory inputs from the retina and then acts as a relay station, thereby processing the sensory information to the visual cortex.

Medial geniculate nucleus functions in the capacity of a relay station for the auditory system.

The thalamus also plays a role in the regulation of consciousness, sleep, and wakefulness.

The intralaminar nuclei are related closely with the process of reticular formation. The strategic positioning of this nuclei allows them to control the level of total activity of the cerebral cortex. The intralaminar nuclei are also able to influence the levels of alertness and consciousness in an individual.

The ventroanterior and ventrolateral nuclei of the thalamus form a part of the basal nuclei circuit and are therefore involved in performing voluntary movements.

Disorders

Sensory Loss

When lesions occur as a result of thrombosis or hemorrhage of one of the arteries that supply the thalamus, sensory loss occurs. Damage to the ventral posterolateral nucleus and the ventral posteromedial nucleus will lead to loss of all the forms of sensation which includes muscle joint sense, light touch, tactile sensation, and discrimination.

Thalamic Cauterization

Cauterizing the intralaminar nuclei result in the relief of severe and intractable pain which is related to terminal cancer.

Degeneration

The hereditary degeneration of thalamus leads to prion disease. Accident to the cerebrovascular results in thalamic syndrome and damage to the mammillary body results in Korsakoff's syndrome.

Full Body Non-Verbal Communication

Body language is an essential part of reading people. As mentioned earlier, people communicate not only through the use of words but also through the use of nonverbal cues of which body language is one. When you are able to identify body languages and are able to tell what they mean, it will be easier for you to analyze people. Body language is used to express emotions and feelings that are expressed, sometimes they occur without the individual thinking of it. It is, therefore, an essential part of communication to understand.

The role of body language is intricate, and it often works with verbal communication in order to create a blunt message. Body language functions in the following capacities:

Regulating

Conflicting

Complementing

Accenting/Moderating

Substituting and

Repeating.

Regulating. This occurs when body language is used to pace and regulate communication. It is used to indicate when the conversation is about to end, and it is another person's turn etc.

Conflicting. This occurs when body language conveys something different from what you are verbally communicating.

Complementing: this is similar to conflicting but with a few differences. Body language is used in an effort to add credibility or support words. If it is genuine, then the message is strengthened, however, if it is perceived as fake, then the message is conflicted.

Accepting/Moderating. This occurs when the individual wants to emphasize, accentuate, enhance or soften what has been communicated verbally

Substituting. This occurs when body language is used to replace verbal communication completely.

Repeating. This occurs when body language is used to repeat the message that has been tried to convey verbally.

There are different forms of body language expressions as a result of the different parts of the body.

The legs and feet

The torso, chest, hips, and shoulders

The arms

The hands and fingers

Facial expressions.

The Legs and Feet

The legs

Legs are an interesting part of communication using nonverbal means as there is a lot to say with our legs without us realizing it. Most times when people attempt to control their body language, they focus on the upper body thereby neglecting the legs, which are able to tell us just what they are thinking. Except for when the upper body and legs are in conflict, and the individual is probably in control.

While open

Standing

Standing with legs apart is a stable stance for people. When the width between the feet is about the width of the shoulders, then the individual is relaxed. A slightly wider width indicates confidence. A wider stance still makes the body appear bigger and wider and indicates power and dominance as it takes up more territory. It shows domination.

Open leg displays make the genitals vulnerable, it could be a sexual display or a show of power. One foot forward with the other behind indicates a frozen walk, i.e. the individual intends to go somewhere.

Sitting

Sitting with slightly open legs indicate relaxedness and comfortability. A wider width can be more of a sexual crotch display. If the individual is a bit worried, they will cover their genitals with their hands.

While closed

Standing

When the feet are together, this may indicate anxiety, it protects the genital., it may also indicate cold. An individual turning slightly to the side, leaning forwards or pulling the hips back indicates an increased desire for protection.

Sitting

The legs may be held together gently or tightly, as a result of the anxiety level.

Crossed

Crossing legs can be used to indicate protectiveness and it can be negative. It may be used to shield the individual from other people and their ideas. This gesture may also indicate a level of tension and anxiety, especially when the legs are held together rigidly and the movements occur more jerkily.

Crossing legs may also be used to indicate shyness and also that the individual needs to visit the toilet.

Pointing

The legs may be used to point to things of interest just like other parts of the body. It can also be used to indicate that the individual needs to leave when it points towards the door or shifts continually. When the leg is pulled back, it is used to indicate disinterest.

Moving

This action helps to exercise the legs and get the blood circulating and also loosen more cramps.

Bouncing the leg may indicate impatience, while pulling it back may show disinterest. It can also swing in time to music indicating relaxedness (and perhaps inviting other people to join in).

When people walk fast, it indicates hurriedness or a determined character, while a slow walk indicates laziness, daydreaming or time to kill.

Longer steps show confidence while shorter ones show timidity or preciseness. A stylish walk, however, indicates self-consciousness.

Striking

Legs can be used as weapons and it indicates aggression.

Touching

The leg can be touched seductively, which indicates a sexual invitation. It may be tapped repeatedly, which indicates impatience or show the individual is in tune with the music.

The feet

Stomping.

When we stomp the feet, we use it to indicate frustration or hostile attitude. It is also used to show that something has gone amiss.

Tapping

The foot can also be tapped and this indicates impatience or boredom. This movement is also used to eliminate some excess energy

Wiggling

When the feet are wiggled or when we rock back and forth on the heels of our feet, we indicate buzzing anticipation and excitement.

The Torso: chest, hips, and shoulders

The torso is also an important part of the body used to communicate nonverbally. It includes the chest, hips, and shoulders and it is able to tell us the things are going through the minds of the individual, without them being aware of it.

The Chest.

Thrust out.

Thrusting the chest out attracts attention and it may be used as a provocative display of romance.

Women thrust out their chest in order to either invite or tease intimate relations. Men do so in order to either display their strong pectoral or hide their bulging gut.

Profile

Standing sideways, exaggerates a thrust out chest. This may be used by women to display the curve of their breasts or by men to display strong profiles.

Withdrawn

When the chest is withdrawn, it may indicate that the individual is trying to hide or appear inoffensive.

Leaning

Leaning the upper body forward may move it closer to another person who may indicate an interest in what the person says or romantic interest in the person.

It can also be used to invade the body space of another person and indicate an aggressive move in a dominant language.

Breathing

The chest moves when the individual breathes. When the breath is deep, the chest moves more and it is thrust out. It also increases oxygen intake and prepares the individual for action, indicating fear or anger. We also breathe deep when we experience emotions intensely.

Breathing fast and deeply (hyperventilating) may indicate anxiety, while difficult and short breaths indicate tension. People in a state of suspense may hold their breath

Touching

When a woman touches her chest in front of a man, it may be considered as a highly suggestive and flirtatious act. And rubbing the chest may be a sign of pain either from tension or stress.

The Shoulders

Raised

When the shoulders are raised with the arms folded together or crossed and hugging the body, it may indicate cold. It may also show tension due to anxiety or fear.

Curved Forward

The body curves forward when the individual's arms are folded. When the body is curved forward with the hands down, it reduces body width and indicates a subconscious desire to not be seen or a defensive posture.

Pushed Back

When the shoulders are pushed back, the chest is thruster out. This is used to show that the individual does not fear attack, and may be used to taunt a demonstration of power.

Circling

Circling the shoulders is a means of exercising a stiff shoulder and may, therefore, indicate anxiety, or that the individual is getting ready for action or combat (for signs of aggression).

Shrugging

This gesture is used to indicate ignorance, or to show that nothing is being concealed. It may also suggest dishonesty when the individual shrugs rather than talk. A more prolonged shrug may indicate aggression, while a shorter one may indicate irritation or frustration.

Relaxed

When the shoulders are held low (relaxed), it indicates that the individual is truly relaxed and the arm can move and swing free.

Leaning

Leaning with the shoulder is a relaxed pose as it does not involve physical movements.

Turning

Turning shoulders is essential to turning away. When this happens when the person looks at you, it indicates disinterest and the desire to leave.

The Hips

Thrust out

The hips contain the primary sexual organs and thrusting them forward indicates a provocative and suggestive gesture. When it is thrust out with the legs open, it suggests an invitation to intercourse. Men may do this as a show of power.

Held back

Holding the hips back protects the genitals and prevents them from detection.

Pushed sideways

Pushing the hips sideways curves the spine and makes the body relax when the individual's body drop. This may indicate disappointment or tiredness. It may also point subtly to what the individual wants. Pointing at someone indicates attraction while pointing at the door indicates the desire to leave.

Moving

Swaying the hips indicates the desire to dance, and it can also be a flirtatious act. Moving the hips back and forth also simulates sexual intercourse and can be arousing.

Touching

Touching the hips push the elbow sideways and make the body seem larger indicating power or aggression. Stroking the hips may also suggest flirtation especially if accompanied by prolonged eye contact and swaying hips.

Hands over the genital indicate fear or embarrassment.

The Arms

Expanded

Arms are parts of our body that can be used to make us appear bigger or smaller. they can also make us reach out without moving other parts of our body. They can be used to extend to the other person in either a show of friendliness or hostility. When they offer comfort or friendliness, they are curved and move more slowly. However, when they are moved directly and quickly, they are threatening.

They can also extend laterally in order to display size and indicate confidence or aggression.

Shaping

They are used as a part of shaping when we wave them around and create the world. They are also used as an adjunct to our words. When we wave them like windmills, it means we are excited or confident while waving in a smaller manner indicates less confidence. A person who bangs their hand while waving may indicate clumsiness.

Raising

Raising arm is used to lift things up, and when it is done quickly enough, it throws things. When it is done in a typical to two-arm raising gesture, it suggests frustration, especially when it is coupled with a shrug.

Weapons

Arms can be used as weapons. They can symbolize clubs and spears and swords when they strike at imaginary foes. They can be used to block, defend and sweep away attacks.

Reaching

When you reach your hand forward, it can be used to indicate support or affection, as you seek to touch and join the other person, while it could also indicate aggression or threat when the arm is thrust forward rapidly especially if the hand rolls into a fist.

Pulling back

When arms are thrust forward, they end up being the first thing to be under attack. Pulling the arm back indicates defensiveness.

Hidden

When arms are placed behind the back, they are hidden from view, which may indicate a hidden intent or concealment. It may be used to either hide something pleasant in order to surprise or something otherwise threatening.

Arms back create vulnerability as it exposes the torso, which can indicate submission or comfort when the individual is with friends or feels powerful enough to be able to withstand sudden attacks.

Crossing

When arms are crossed, they form a closed and defensive shield that blocks the outside world out. These shields are to either block out incoming signals, or a place to hide and not be noticed. When arms are crossed, they can also indicate anxiety which can be as a result of an internal discomfort and a sense of vulnerability or as a lack of trust in some other person.

The extent to which the individual crosses the arms suggests how closed the person is. This could range from crossing lightly to folding arms to wrapping arms around the person. When the arms are crossed tightly with fingers clenched tightly to form a fist, it may be used to indicate hostility.

If the crossing is in a self-hug, it indicates self-reassurance. When arms are crossed especially when trying to hold one another, it may be to suppress signals and also to indicate repressed anger.

When arms are crossed in a folded position, it may indicate comfort. When arms are not crossed, it exposes the torso making the individual vulnerable, it indicates comfort and trust.

Arms are crossed when the individual is cold and when arms are crossed in front of other people, it suggests disinterest and rejection.

Hugging

Arms are also predominantly used in hugging, which indicates affection.

The Hands and Fingers

The Hands

Holding

When hands are cupped together or over an item, it symbolizes delicacy or holding a fragile idea. They may also be involved in giving.

Gripping items may indicate ownership, desire, and possessiveness. Hands may also be used to hold the self, for comfort, or as an act of restraint, it also indicates nervousness. Wringing the hands together may indicate extreme nervousness. The tightness of holding may indicate the degree of tension an individual is feeling.

Holding hands behind the back can be used to express trust and confidence, it may also be used to conceal the hands displaying tension. The two hands may conflict each other, an example is one forms a fist and the other restrains it.

Holding imaginary objects when talking about them shows importance. Important things are held close while unwanted things are held far away. When hands are clenched together in front of the person in a relaxed manner with the individual moving the thumb upwards, pleasure is indicated.

Control

A hand with the palms down may be used to figuratively hold a person down thereby indicating authority, or as a request, Palms down indicates dominance. Pushing the palm outward towards others or items fends them off or pushes them away. A pointing finger or hand can instruct an individual to leave.

Greetings

Opening the palm indicates no concealed weapon.

Dominance is expressed during greeting (handshakes) with hand on top, prolonged holding or strength and also by holding the other person with the free hand.

Affection is expressed with the speed and length of a handshake, touching with the other hand and enthusiastic smiles.

Submission is expressed with palm up, floppy and sometimes clammy hand and quick withdrawal.

Equality is shown with vertical handshakes, firm without being crushing and lasting an exact period.

Hands are also involved in waving for distance, and salutes as well, but in the military

Shaping

Hands are used to carve the air and create visual metaphors out of nothing.

Covering

Hands are used to hide objects. Hand over the ear is used to block sound out, hand over the eye is used to block sight. Hand over the mouth is used to prevent talk.

Hands covering mouth while speaking may indicate lying or uncertainty. It is also used to hide blushing, swallowing and tension.

Hands are placed at the heart to protect it from shocking harm, or to the groin to protect from dangerous attack.

Giving

Outstretched hands are involved in giving other people items.

Asking

Palm offered upwards indicates a plea gesture. Palm downwards indicate asking a person to calm down. Palms up or at 45 degrees and pulled to the body indicates bring others closer.

Hands with palms pressed together indicate an anxious pleading; when the fingers point upward, it indicates a prayer position; when fingers are pointed down, it indicates a less anxious desire to agree.

Rubbing

Rubbing the hands together may indicate cold. It may also indicate glee. Doing this slowly and bless obviously may indicate benefiting at the expense of others. Massaging hands together indicate stress or anxiety.

Rubbing the face and chin may indicate thinking and evaluating. It is also used to relieve soreness or tension or to indicate romantic invitation when the body is stroked.

Thinking

When the fingers are placed together in a steeple, pointing upwards, it indicates confidence and superiority over others. When the hands are pressed together more, it indicates more tension and hope. When the fingers are intertwined and held under the chin, it indicates thinking and evaluating. When hands are clenched, it may indicate self-restraint.

Touching

Touching oneself may indicate self-affirmation and related anxiety. It is also used in romantic situations. It could also be a form of punishment, like slapping someone on the head.

Touching someone on the shoulder while telling them off indicates authority, while a gentle touch on the arm indicates sympathy and concern.

Preening

Preening may indicate feelings of vulnerability or an air of superiority.

Weighing

Cupping hands may be used to indicate importance.

Trembling

When someone's hands tremble, it often indicates fright or excitement. Dropping things, however, may indicate a loss of control.

The fingers

Point

Fingers are used to indicate direction; long distance has the finger pointing directly upward. The thumb may be used to point to something when it is jerked over the shoulder.

Club

The finger is used in admonition when it beats up and down at people. When it is pointed downward, it sometimes indicates something important. When the forefinger is held up and stationary, it means to wait.

Prod

The finger is used to prod, stabbing forward at a person like a stiletto knife. It is also used to prod downwards at an imaginary item.

Plate

When the fingers are extended and closed with the palm, it forms a plate, or it could form a cup which may indicate symbolic things such as ideas.

Drumming or Tapping

When the fingers are used to drum or tap, it indicates frustration, or the desire to leave a gathering.

Thumbs-up and Thumbs-down

The thumbs-up sign is used to indicate approval while the thumbs-down sign indicates disapproval. When it is held sideways or wagged, it indicates uncertainty.

Crossed fingers indicate hope. Sucking fingers is used to indicate feelings of inferiority and timidity.

When the fingernails are inspected or fidgeted, it indicates boredom and disinterest.

When fingers are fluttered, it may indicate uncertainty

Facial expressions

Facial expressions are essential for communicating nonverbally, just like other body parts. They are perhaps the most obvious nonverbal means of communicating nonverbal and the easiest to hide. They are also among the universal forms of body language. They are used to express happiness, fear, sadness, anger around the universe. Other emotions they are able to express include contempt, disgust, surprise and more. It is also possible to make judgments on the intelligence of individuals based on their facial expressions.

The eyes

The eyes are referred to as the "window to the soul" as they can reveal a great deal about people. Taking note of eye movements is essential when conversing with other people. While evaluating facial expressions, pay attention to:

Pupil Size

This is a very subtle way of communicating nonverbally. Although, the level of light in the environment control pupil dilation, emotions could also lead to changes in pupil size. Highly dilated eyes can be used to indicate that a person is aroused or interested.

Blinking

This gesture is natural, however, the frequency at which it occurs is what matters i.e. blinking too much or too little. When people blink too fast, it may indicate the feeling of distress or discomfort. Infrequent blinking may suggest that the person is deliberately trying to control the eye movements.

Eye Gaze

When an individual looks directly into your eyes during a conversation, it suggests that the person is interested and pays attention. However, when eye contact is prolonged, it may indicate threats. Breaking eye contact and looking away frequently, might suggest that the individual is uncomfortable or distracted or trying to hide what he or she truly feels.

The Mouth

While evaluating facial expressions, pay attention to the following clues in the mouth:

Pursed lips. When the lips are pursed or tightened, it may suggest distaste, distrust or disapproval.

Covering the mouth. When the mouth is covered, it is often used to hide an emotional reaction or to avoid displaying smiles or smirks.

Lip Biting. Sometimes when people bite their lips, it suggests that they are worried, stressed or anxious. Chewing on the lower lip, however, indicates worry, fear or insecurity.

Smiling. When it is genuine, it indicates happiness or satisfaction, however, when it is false, it indicates false happiness, cynicism or sarcasm.

Mouth turned up or down. Slight changes made in the mouth can also be used to indicate in a subtle manner what a person is feeling. When the mouth is slightly turned up, it might indicate the feeling of happiness or optimism. On the other hand, when the mouth is slightly turned down, it indicates sadness, grimace or disapproval.

The body languages described above are only some of the several body languages expressed by the body. There are so many and in order for the individual to be able to analyze people successfully, he or she must be aware and take cognizance of the different body languages.

Avoiding Danger: Detecting deception

Danger exists in all forms and manners, even in your bid to know how to analyze people. Perhaps, you are unable to analyze the individual accurately, when you think you have done the analysis perfectly, this could prove to be dangerous. For instance, if there ever is a time when you would be required to take actions and escape danger by accurately analyzing and reading the people you are involved with, and you what you analyzed turned out to be wrong because you have been deceived, the danger would only be enhanced. There are several forms in which dangers exist.

One of the ways where you can avoid dangers or harmful situations is by detecting when you are being lied to and deceived accurately, without fail, because your safety might be dependent on it.

Deception Detection

Research has consistently shown that even though people believe in their ability to detect lies and deceptions, the ability in real life is no more accurate than chance or flipping a coin. Especially, during the investigation of crime when it is important for law enforcement agents to detain the criminals without complicating innocent suspects. This is however tough enough because the search for truth is not easy, and "there really is no Pinocchio's nose."

Several types of research have been conducted on the nonverbal signs attached with deception based on the belief that concealing deception is difficult, since:

it takes more mental effort to tell lies and deceive than it takes to tell the truth,

emotions are said to give people away when they are deceptive, lying leads to more stress and anxiety.

However, people only think that the signs of deception should be obvious to the world through their nonverbal behavior or body language since they are hard to control. Research shows that people that lie are more prone to:

fidget more often

make their responses shorter than normal

blink more often

make more speech errors, such as umm, ah's, and eh's.

It should, however, be noted that the researchers found that:

People that lie rarely or do not break eye contact when they are lying.

These people, in a similar way as truth-telling people would, are likely to "look you in the eye."

Using nonverbal behaviors in detecting deception is not the most effective method of detecting deception.

Why is it difficult to detect deception through nonverbal behaviors?

It is essential to note that it is totally possible to detect deception through nonverbal behaviors because genuine feelings and emotions do leak or become displayed unconsciously. However, these genuine displays, which are referred to as micro expressions do not last long, just about a fraction of a second. As a result of this, they are usually too brief to be noticed and to make any conclusions from.

Furthermore, the nonverbal clues that are often identified represent the things that might happen when studying several individuals and not what the specific individual is more likely to do. An example of this situation is such that, in a sample of 500 men, it is found that there are more whites than there are Hispanics. When a particular individual is selected, there is no way to know certainly if the individual is white or Hispanic. It may be expected that individuals who tell lies stutter and are unable to clearly speak when they are telling lies, however, this may not be so for all liars. Some of them might itch their chin and display other cues, but not stutter.

Also, the nonverbal cues that are found are based on small patterns, they are not particularly strong and informative differences. An example of this instance is when there is a large group of people involving both male and female of particular heights. However, the average difference in heights is very small, say about less than half of an inch. This difference is regarded as the statistical difference, however, it is so small, it can be neglected. It is less useful when it is used to determine the sex of an individual based on their height. When an individual who tells lies is questioned, it might be expected that he would blink his eyes while replying and lying, however, it is a fact that both truth-tellers and liars blink their eyes while talking, except liars blink more times than truth-tellers when talking. However, some liars rarely blink while some truth-tellers blink a lot.

Essentially, it has been discovered that small statistical differences exist in detection cues, thereby making it extremely difficult to generalize as liars or truth-tellers based on the cues that have been identified.

Reasons why the identified nonverbal cues are not effective in detecting deception

The truth-tellers and liars are more similar in the way they act and do things more than they are different.

Several of the lies told by people are often not planned for, they usually come naturally without thought or effort. They are often effortless and automatic. Several people are not aware of them telling lies when they do it, so, deception can come across as natural to some people because for them, it is.

Sometimes, however, people feel stress or anxiety when they tell lies, but a good number of times, they tell the same sets of lies over and over. For this reason, people become comfortable with the lies with the passage of time, and may actually begin to believe the lie.

More often than not, telling the truth may be as difficult and stressful as lying, even more than. You could have experienced the feeling of agitation, confusion, anxiety or even been upset when you were trying to tell the truth, only to have the people doubt the things you are saying. Important situations are stressful for both liars and truth-tellers, and in such situation, the two teams can get nervous, such that they will both be regarded as telling lies.

There are strategies, that involves both verbal and nonverbal communication, and is used to spot a lie and it can sometimes be conflicting or even confusing. The following include some of the signs and strategies that are used to detect deception:

A change in Voice

A retired FBI criminal profiler, Gregg McCrary states that the voice and mannerism of an individual are bound to change when they tell lies. This criminal profiler takes the strategy of identifying the regular speech patterns and mannerisms of the liar by asking typical and easy questions such as the name of the person and where the individual lives. This speech pattern and mannerisms is compared with the change that may occur in speaking or mannerisms when more challenging and interrogative questions are asked.

They may try to remain still.

This may seem weird but being perfectly still or remaining still is an indicator for people who do not tell the truth. The movement of such people is usually minimized. They might even pull their arms and legs in towards their body, which is an indication of being tense or nervous. Think about it, people generally feel more relaxed when things are normal, and they may express more fluidity and movement in their body. However, when things are awry, such as when the individual has to tell a white lie or a huge fib, the body might become rigid or stiff and the individual may be unable to move.

Body expressions may not match what is said out loud

Have you ever witnessed a situation where a person tells another person that everything is fine when the body language expressed states something different? That is a sign that things are not alright and they are not telling the truth to even themselves. Sometimes, it happens that when an individual is lying, the timing between the things they are saying and their expressions may be off or the expressions may not match their words. Imagine asking an individual a question and such a person shakes his/her head and says yes. Or presenting an "I am sorry" card and a big bouquet of flower to someone while frowning.

Their language can change

When people lie, they may make use of a language that distance them from the truth and may even change the selection of pronouns they use when they speak, such that "I misplaced his wallet," may become "I misplaced the wallet," in a bid to show that they have less connection to the object(s) and to the items being discussed.

Also, truth-tellers often make use of the pronoun "I" in describing their actions, such as in the statement: "I woke up by 6:30, I want to the bathroom to brush my teeth and have my bath, when I was done, I heard the phone ringing, so I had to walk to the kitchen to answer it. I then fed my cat and attempted to eat some cereals myself and that was when I realized that my TV was missing from the living room." The above statement contains the pronoun "I" several times.

Deceptive people, however, often use language that reduces the references made to themselves, this is done by describing events using the passive voice. This includes:

"The door was open" instead of "I left the door open."

"The safe was left unlocked" instead of "I left the safe unlocked."

Another way by which self-references can be reduced is by substituting the pronoun "you" for "I."

Question: Can you tell me about the money?

Answer: You know, sometimes when you need to live, you just need to get out there and you do what needs to be done. You just have to..."

When oral statements or informally written statements are made, deceptive statements often omit the self-referencing pronouns. The following is a statement made by a husband who claimed the wife was accidentally killed: "I picked up the gun to clean it. Moved it to the left hand to get the cleaning rod. Something bumped the trigger. The gun went off, hitting my wife."

Although the man acknowledged that he picked the gun up, he however omitted "I" in the second sentence and in the third sentence, he substitutes "I" for "something." The man referred to "the" gun and "the" left hand instead of my gun and my left hand.

Equivocation

The subject is prone to avoid the questions of the interviewer by filling the sentences s/he makes with weak modifiers, expressions of uncertainty and vague expressions. You should, therefore, watch out for words such as guess, sort of, think, might, approximately, about, perhaps, could, maybe etc. When vague statements and expressions of uncertainty are made, they give the deceptive person leeway to modify the assertions made at a later time, without directly being in conflict with the original statement made.

Noncommittal verbs include: think, believe, guess, figure, assume, suppose, etc.

Equivocating adjectives and adverbs include sort of, about, maybe, perhaps, almost, mainly etc.

Vague qualifiers include: you might say, more or less etc.

Answering questions with questions

Even liars would rather not lie, because telling lies out rightly makes the risk of deception greater. Instead of lying, the deceptive person would rather avoid answering the question asked altogether, and a common way of avoiding questions is to reply with a question of your own. You should, therefore, be alert when you hear responses such as:

"Do I seem like I could ever do something like that?"

"Do you think I am stupid enough to remove cash from my own register drawer?"

Oaths

Deceptive people attempt to provide as little useful information as is possible to their questioner, they also attempt very hard to convince the questioner that the replies they have given are true. This might involve making use of mild oaths in order to make their statements more convincing. Deceptive people are more likely to add certain expressions to their statements. These expressions include: "I swear," "I cross my heart," "as God is my witness," etc. Truthful individuals, however, are more convicted in their statement and they require no fact in proving the veracity of their statements, therefore, they feel less need to support their statements with oaths.

Taking that hardline pause

Deceptive people may take several pauses during the course of their statement as they create the details or stories in their head, or describe their actions using circumstances that never existed. Paying attention to these pauses may be important because it could be that the individual is attempting to make up events on-the-go. Additionally, people who are engaged in this behavior i.e. they take pauses during the course of conversing with them may exhibit behaviors that are in line with deceptive people.

Euphemism

Several languages offer alternative terms for virtually all actions or situations. When deceptive people make statements, they often include mild or vague words in deceiving their actions rather than the harsher and more explicit synonyms. Euphemisms are bound to portray the behavior of the liar in a more favorable light and reduce the harm the actions of the subjects led to. When you are communicating with liars, watch out for such terms as "missing" instead of "stolen," "bumped" instead of "hit," "borrowed" instead of "took," and "warned" instead of "threatened."

Alluding to Actions

People often allude to certain actions without actually stating in explicit terms, that they perform them. This is also common in deceptive people. Consider the following statement from someone questioned on the loss of some important data: "I always try to back up my computer and put away my papers every day before I leave for home. Last Tuesday, I decided to copy my files onto the network drive, like I always do, then I started putting my files into my desk drawer. I also decided to lock the list of customers in the office safe." The above statement stated what she always did, but on that particular Tuesday, if you notice, she did not state that:

she backed up her computer

copied her files onto the network drive.

put her files into her desk drawer

locked the customer list in the office safe.

She alluded to all the actions, without being definite about taking part in any of them. You should be attentive and careful and make sure that you do not assume when people do not state explicitly.

Pointing your Fingers

The act of pointing towards a person or an object may indicate the desire to shift the focus from an individual onto someone or something else. This is however based on the premise that the individual either gesticulates normally or not, which will be determined using a baseline (described above). Also, if they point their finger in a direction other than the direction their eyes are focused on, they could be deceiving you.

Lack of Detail

When statements are true, they often contain specific details, some of these details may not even be relevant to the conversation. This is because truth-tellers retrieve their statements from the long-term memory, which stores several facts about each experience, such as - the new pants you were wearing at the time, the intensity of the sun, the music playing in the background and much more. Some of these details are bound to show up when the statement made by the individual is truthful.

Deceptive people, however, fabricate a story and are prone to keep their statements simple and brief. Few liars have imaginations that can make up detailed descriptions of events that did not happen. A deceptive person, however, wants to reduce the risk that the person he or she is conversing with may at some point discover proof that is contradictory to certain aspects of the statements they have made., therefore, the fewer the facts that might be proved to be wrong, the better.

Mean Length of Utterance

The average number of words that can be uttered per sentence is referred to as the "mean length of sentence." (MLU)

The MLU is equal to the total number of words in a statement divided by the number of sentences made.

MLU = Total number of words / Total number of sentences

Majority of the people tend to speak in sentences that have between 10 and 15 words. When people, however, are anxious about an issue, they tend to speak in sentences that are either substantially shorter or substantially longer than what is regarded as the norm. You should, therefore, pay special attention to the sentences whose length is significantly different from the MLU of the people you are talking to.

How to be a Better Reader

Being able to analyze people can be a hard nut to crack, as it requires a lot of mental work. From studying the body languages to understanding facial expressions, and how to manage the emotions expressed by people and their egos. It takes a huge amount to analyze people. However, the mental work and activities required can only be possible if you are able to read people, and not just read, you have to be excellent at it too.

The ability and capacity to be able to read people is something that you have to develop with constant practice, and it is just like every other thing in the world, some people are much better at it than other people. Quite naturally, the people who have acquired knowledge, combined with real-world practice are essentially the best people at it. Reading people is a natural act and humans being social creatures are wired to read and study people every time we interact with each other.

People are involved in the proceedings of this world and in studying them, they could either cooperate or not want to. However, even when people think they are not giving you the chance to study them in order to be able to analyze them better, they still are. Sitting alone in the corner of the room away from everyone also requires cooperation on some level with the society.

For instance, some nations are not attempting to war each other, because of the interconnected network of human behavior designed to instill peace and harmony functions as it should. Therefore, it is essentially the cooperation and behavior of several people cooperating together on some level by essentially, keeping away from participating in acts that might lead to harm in another person,

People are not as good as they think they are

When you come in contact with a stranger, how long does it take you to evaluate the individual before you arrive at your first impression?

Several people believe it took them less than a minute to do this, however, science has found that it takes a lot less time than people believe it to be. Psychologists at Princeton University have established through several studies on the subject that it takes an individual only about one-tenth of a second to make the first judgment of someone, and it is primarily based on the body language of the other person.

Dr. Albert Mehrabian discussed a fact in one of his books that only about 7% of communication is made through the use of words, while the remaining 93% is as a result of vocal clues and nonverbal messages such as posture, gestures and facial expressions among others.

Simply put, you need to be aware of the way people come across to you and how you come across to them, as they form the vast majority of human interaction. Being able to identify these cues could either make or break the career of a budding professional.

If you are looking to move up the ladder in a social situation, be it at work, in your community etc., you have to be able to harness the knowledge of body language and nonverbal cues, as they provide you with a huge advantage in both professional and non-professional circumstances. The ability to speed-read, and analyze people accurately could be what stands between you impressing the people you look up to and embarrassing the people around you.

All of these, however, brings to mind an important question, how exactly can you improve your ability to read people?

What are you doing wrong?

Before we go on to answer the question "how to improve your ability to read people?" We first need to establish the things you are doing wrong, so that these discrepancies will cease to come up, and you will be able to read people better.

There are some common errors that people make in a bid to understand people and read them better. These errors may include:

Ignoring Context. This is an important fact people tend to overlook. The context in which the nonverbal clue is bring expressed do matter a lot. The fact that you have your arms crossed, do not necessarily indicate that the room is cold or the chair you are sitting on does not have armrests. A good number of times, things have to go beyond the common sense situations attached to the environment. It is therefore essential to ask yourself the question: "Should someone in this situation act in this manner?" You should remember that the arms might be crossed in a bid to fend off danger or simply to hide, or protect the torso, it might be crossed in order for the individual to self-reassure his/herself, or because the individual is angry. Always make sure to include the context in which the individual is exhibiting these cues.

Not looking for clusters. This happens to be one of the biggest mistakes you can make. Looking for a single tell might be great in movies, but it is different in real life. In real life, it is more about a consistent grouping of actions. An example of such is the case of poker players, rather than the single tell described in movies, a consistent grouping of actions which include sweating, touching the face and stuttering together describes what you might find, to be meaningful. It is therefore essential to ask the question: Are most of the behaviors exhibited by this person associated with "X"? For instance, an angry person will not cross his arms alone, he would probably frown and fume and exhibit a group of behaviors that will indicate anger.

Not establishing a baseline. Baselines are essential if you are to know for certain the nonverbal and verbal behaviors exhibited by an individual. The fact that the individual is jumpy does not indicate anything. However, if the individual is always jumpy and then suddenly stops moving, you should ask yourself the question: "Is this the normal way they act?" When you do not establish a baseline with which new behaviors can be compared, it will be difficult to understand and ascertain if the behavior being exhibited is normal to the individual, or not.

Not being conscious of Biases. The first impression you make of an individual is bound to affect your judgment of the person. If you already like or dislike, the individual, then you are bound to judge based on it. If the people who come close to you and often compliment you are the same people you like and approve of, it just might sway you unconsciously. It will also be a long while before you can become impressed by people you do not approve of. (Saying these tricks do not apply to you is also a bias. The biggest bias of all occurs when you think you are unbiased).

Why is it important to know how to read people?

Being able to read people comes with its benefits and it is so much more than playing Sherlock Holmes. It is about observing the people you communicate with and adjusting the manner with which you communicate with them.

In every area of life, there are a myriad of personality types to deal with, and it is essential to be able to recognize them if we are going to tap into their strengths. For instance, if you have an employee or a friend you observe to have low self-esteem or lacks self-confidence, you should be able to adjust your tone in order to accommodate their insecurities in a way that motivates them. It would be wrong and inefficient if you were to be loud and boisterous in your manner of dealing with them. However, if the individual you are dealing with is an extrovert, then being solemn and serious is an inefficient way of getting through to them.

The world of today disconnects us from one another and even nature than ever before. Today, we hardly make eye-contact with the barista who hands us our coffee over the counter. The power of observation and the need to read people accurately is therefore not necessary for communicating effectively. It is only a tool that helps to promote the connection between us as human beings.

Reading People

The ability to read people has more to do with nonverbal communication and body language alone. The essential things to look at before you can successfully read people include posture, gestures, physical movements, the person's appearance, facial expressions, the tone of voice and willingness to make eye contact during conversations etc. There is a study that finds that you can read someone only 7% from the words they say, 38% from their vocal clue, such as tone, pitch and volume and finally, 55% from their body language. The study was however focused on reading someone on a first impression basis.

You also have to consider the context in which the behaviors are being exhibited, personality and the possibility that anybody might try to deceive you by manipulating the communication.

These clues, however, do not make you privy to the innermost thoughts and feelings of other people, however, if you are observant, then you will be able to read their body language. The following include some steps to take in order to be able to read people better.

Establish a baseline

Majority of people have different behavioral quirks and sometimes these quirks are habitual. Examples include clearing their throat, scratching their head, stroking their necks and so on. It is, however, essential that you read and understand what the normal behavior of the person is, and that is your baseline

Know the person. In order to be able to read a person better, you have to establish a baseline and to establish a baseline, you have to know the person well. By getting to know them personally, you are going to have a better idea of the things they like and dislike, their behavioral habits etc. Also, you have to pay attention to the individuals and their habits, even the littlest habits, such as eye gaze, fluttering the eyes etc. This will help you in noting the things to look for when you are analyzing them.

It is essential then to base your opinions of other people on several of your encounters with them, not just one because sometimes situations determine the actions and mannerisms of everyone. For instance, one of your friends may be very fidgety. Fidgeting would normally be a sign of nervousness or dishonesty, but in this individual, it is a natural habit. If you had not been the friend of the individual and just came across them on the street, your impression of them would be nervous or anxious which in reality is wrong.

Ask open-ended questions. During the process of reading someone, what you are doing is watching and listening. What you are not doing, however, is taking control of the conversation and steering it in your direction. Ask your question straight and make your conclusions. Open-ended questions will give the individual room to talk more, allowing you to observe them for a longer time. When you ask questions that are not straight to the point, you may get a rambling reply that may not provide you with adequate information.

Look for inconsistencies in their baseline. It is also important to seek out the discrepancies in the baseline. For instance, when a normally affectionate person turns out to not be physically present anymore and does not seem to want to be close to anyone, then you should know that something is up with such person. Once you identify the individual's daily pattern of behavior, be on the lookout for events or behaviors that stand out. In the example of the affectionate person, when you ask why s/he suddenly becomes aloof, you may find that it is because they: are exhausted, got in a fight with other people, or other personal issues that bothers them.

Work in Clusters. Identifying only one cue is not enough reason to make conclusions. For instance, someone could lean away from you because the chair on which they are sitting is hard to be comfortable in. Even if you are focused on their nonverbal behavior, make sure to identify between three and four different signs before you make conclusions. You can take a cue from their tone, their body, their face, and their words. If you can get one from each, then it may be safe to make assumptions.

Identify your own weaknesses. "It is the nature of man to err." This statement indicates the vulnerability of human and their fallibility. Everybody likes pretty things, even the Pope, and the odds are when you identify something as pretty, you are going to like it, even if the something "pretty" is dangerous. As humans, we generally think of the drunks that roam the street with a knife as dangerous, when in reality, most psychopaths are charming and orderly. Even though it is virtually impossible to control this thought of yours, be aware of the tendency your subconscious possess to have you judge a book by its cover when it may not be the best or most accurate thing to do.

Register Vocal Cues.

It is important that you pay attention to the vocal cues exhibited by the individual during the course of your conversation.

Listen to the tone of voice. The voice of an individual is enough to tell you about the way the individual feels. Watch out for the inconsistencies that may arise in their tone or the pitch of their voice. Do they sound angry and happy? Do they sound tired and happy? If the answer to these questions is yes, then they are probably making attempts to cover things up.

When paying attention to the voice, note the volume also, do they talk louder or quieter than is normal for them? Also, watch out for such expressions as "um" or "uh," do they use them often? If the answer is yes, again, then the individual might be nervous or lying and delaying. Make sure to note if their tone, however, transmits an emotion they are not expressing totally. For example, do these people sound angry or sarcastic? They may feel the need to address what is going on in a passive manner.

Note the tone and length of their responses. When the responses you are being offered are short and clipped, it could mean that the individual is either busy or frustrated. If the responses are, however, long, then that means that the person is interested and would like to go on with the conversation.

Consider the choice of words. When people talk about things, there is often a process behind the content. For instance, if a friend said to you, you are dating another nurse?" The fact that they used the word "another" suggests that what they really mean is "Oh, but you just dated a nurse and see where that led to, now you are dating another one."

Of recent, people have used the construction "yeah, no." These two words indicate ambivalence and are also used to indicate definiteness, assent or dissent or anything at all. If your friend says to you, Dude, Come on." The "dude" in the statement indicates solidarity by saying, friend. Begin analyzing the words of the individual in order to indicate how they feel truly.

Reading people in different contexts.

There are different contexts in which you communicate with people. All contexts, however, require you to analyze the other person in order to become more connected and understand then better. The way you would read your partner on a date would be different from the way you would read your interviewer.

Know the appropriate clues in a romantic context. When you are on a date, you might want to be sure that the other person is attracted to you and also, is interested in you., again it is essential to read the clues in clusters and not as one. It is a common occurrence for people, especially women, to be mistaken as being interested when they are only friendly, so stay alert and watch out for the clues.

Watch out for the body language they exhibit. Do they lean forward? Is their body language relaxed (i.e. are their arms not crossed or shoulders tensed)? When these signs are present, it shows that the person feels comfortable with you and is probably interested in you. Also, try to notice the frequency with which the other person talks and how immersed they are in the conversation. If they are interested in the conversation, they would nod when you talk, lean forward and ask questions. Also, notice the rate at which they smile, if they, however, seem tense and do not smile the entire time, it may suggest that they do not feel comfortable. At the end of the day, notice how they approach you. It is at this time that you should be aware of interactions that deal with touch., as this will give you an insight into how they feel towards you.

Know the constructs of a job interview. Partaking in a job interview can be nerve-wracking and at the end of it all, it is often difficult to ascertain how well one performed. You should keep an eye out for body languages, as they may mean that the interview is going on well. However, also know that in this context, both the interviewer and interviewee are alert. You might want to watch out for body languages such as the interviewer leaning in and asking questions. You want them to show that they are interested in you and the things you have to say. However, if your interviewer shuffle papers, check his or her phone or computer screen, this may suggest that they are losing interest. You should attempt to recapture their attention if they appear to be getting impatient or bored.

After the interview and you are about to leave, notice how the interviewer says goodbye to you. Do they shake you firmly and with a genuine smile? If yes, then it may mean that the interview went well.

Listen to your Intuition.

Intuition refers to what your gut feels and not what your head says. Intuition is a piece of nonverbal information where you perceive via images, body knowing and "ah-has" rather than logic. In a bid to understand someone, what counts most is who the person is on the inside, not what they look like on the outside. Intuition allows you to see further than what is obvious.

Honor your gut feelings. Listen to what your gut tells you, especially during initial meetings. Listen to the visceral reactions that occur before you get a chance to think. Gut feelings are primal responses and they occur quickly. They are your internal truth meter and they help you decide if you can trust people.

Feel the Goosebumps. Goosebumps are intuitive tingles which informs us that we resonate with individuals who inspire us or are saying something that we can relate to. Goosebumps also occur when you experience deja-vu.

Watch out for intuitive empathy. Sometimes, you are able to feel the physical symptoms and emotions present in your own body. This feeling is intense empathy. Notice the feeling of empathy you experience during conversations with people and obtain feedback.

Pay attention to flashes of insight. During your conversations with people, you may get an "ah-ha moments" about people and it often comes in a flash. It is essential that you remain alert, otherwise, you might miss it. However, we tend to move on to the next thought so rapidly, we lose critical thoughts.

Bonding with people through body language

As humans, it is in our nature to desire to create a connection with people, and it is for this reason that lacking in healthy personal relationships can be detrimental to our health, both mentally and emotionally. Learning to create a connection with other people helps you establish a rapport with them rapidly

The signals we send out through our body language might not be the first thing we think of when we meet someone however, they may exert a powerful effect on the other person. The human brain has been designed to pay attention to the several nonverbal cues that are exhibited by other people, even if it is not consciously. Being able to bond with others through the body language gives us an inkling into what their mind is like and why they do things the way they do it. When we bond through body language, it allows us to be aware of the power beneath the signals and understand them better.

One of the essential ways of bonding through the use of body language is by "Mirroring."

Mirroring

Mirroring is essentially a social phenomenon that requires one person mimicking the gestures, postures, and words of another person. A good number of times, we are not aware of when this phenomenon occurs, however, it is a sign that people are becoming more attuned to -and in sync with- each other. Mirroring body language is a way that allows people to bond with each other and build understanding.

The most obvious form by which people mirror each other include yawning and smiling. Virtually everyone yawns and smiles, and when you see someone yawn or even only read the word yawn, you are more likely going to yawn either immediately, or within the next couple of seconds. It was once believed that the purpose of yawning was to oxygenate the body, but now it has been found that yawning serves as a form of mirroring in order to create rapport and bond with others and also to avoid aggression.

Smiling can also be considered to be contagious because when you see a person smiling, it makes you want to smile too thereby feeling better, even if you were not feeling happy at the time.

According to some scientists, there is a particular neuron in the brain that stimulates the parts of the brain that is in charge of recognizing faces and facial expressions. This neuron allows you to mirror the looks on their faces. It allows you to copy the facial expression of other people.

Mirroring body language is a nonverbal means of conveying the message "I am like you. We are exactly the same I feel the same way you do and we share the same attitudes." It is for this reason that people at a rock concert jump to their feet and applaud simultaneously. The synchronicity of the crowd provides a secure feeling among the participants and enhance it. It is also for this same reason that people in an angry mob will mirror aggressive attitudes and why people who are often calm lose their cool and join the mob. Research has shown that when people experience the same emotions, they are more likely to experience other emotions such as trust, connection and understanding mutually. They will also begin to mirror their facial expressions and body language.

Another situation in which mirroring works is in a queue. In a queue, people are willing to simply cooperate with other people, even though they have never met them before and probably will never meet them again. They are, however, willing to obey an unwritten set of behavioral rules while they wait for an art gallery, in a bank, or in war. From the University of Michigan, Professor Joseph Heinrich found that the urge to mirror other people are simply hardwired into the brain because when people cooperate, it leads to better health, more food and economic growth for the community and the members of the community. It also provides an explanation for the reason why societies with high discipline in mirroring, which includes, British, ancient Romans and Germans dominated the world for several years.

When you mirror the body language and appearance of another person, it shows a united front and it does not allow one person to cheat the other.

Mirroring also makes other people feel at ease. It is such a strong tool for building bonds such that slow-motion video reveals that mirroring extends to such actions such as blinking, raising the eyebrow, nostril-flaring, and even pupil dilation. This is remarkable, because, these gestures are micro and cannot be imitated consciously.

Creating the Right Vibes

Studies made into synchronous body behavior reveals that people who feel the same emotions or are on the same emotional level and, are likely to be establishing a bond will begin to mirror the body language and the expressions of one another. The phenomenon of being on the same wavelength in order to bond with another person begins early from the womb when our heartbeat and body functions match the rhythm of that of our mothers.

During the early stages of courtship, it is common to see people behave in a manner synchronous to each other, almost as if they are dancing. An example of this is when a man takes a mouthful of food and the woman wipes the corner of her mouth, or he begins a sentence and she finishes it for him.

When people say that they "feel right" or that "the vibes are right" around another person, they unknowingly refer to synchronous behavior and mirroring. For instance, when at a restaurant, an individual may feel reluctant to eat or drink alone because they do not want to be out of sync with the other people. And when it is time for them to order their meal, they may check what the others are ordering before they order.

Mirroring on a Cellular Level

Dr. Memhet Oz, an American heart surgeon reports some findings from heart recipients. He found that the heart seems to retain cellular memories in a similar manner as other body organs. This may allow some patients to experience some of the emotions that were experienced by the heart donor. He also found that some recipients assume gestures and postures similar to that of the donor even though they have never been in contact with the donor. He concluded, stating that it may seem like the heart cells instruct the brain of the recipient to take on the body language of the donor.

Conversely, individuals who suffer from disorders such as autism lack the ability to mirror the behavior of other people, thereby making it difficult for them to engage Ina two-way communication with others. This same phenomenon applies to drunk people, whose gestures are often out of sync with the things they say, thereby making it impossible for mirroring to occur.

Due to the phenomenon of cause and effect, when you deliberately assume certain body language positions, you will begin to experience certain emotions that are related to those gestures. For instance, if you are feeling confident, you are likely to unconsciously assume the steeple pose, in order to reflect what you feel. However, if you assume the steeple pose intentionally, then you are likely to feel confident and have other people begin to perceive you as being confident. It then becomes a powerful tool to establish bonds and create a rapport with other people by intentionally matching and mirroring their body language and posture.

Mirroring Differences Between Women and Men

At the University of Manchester, Geoffrey Beattie found that a woman is instinctively about four times more likely to mirror another woman than it is for a man to mirror another man. The man also found that women mirror and match the body language of men also, however, men are reluctant to mirror the gestures or postures of women, except the man is in a courtship mode.

When a woman says that she is able to "see' that someone does not agree with the opinion of the group, she actually "sees" the disagreement, because the woman is able to pick up when the body language of an individual is out of sync with that of the group and they show this disagreement by not mirroring the body language of the group. The way women "see" disagreements, dishonesty, anger, hurt and so on has always been an issue that amazes most men. This is because the brain of most men are not well equipped to read all the details, especially the subtle and tiny details of the body language of other people, and they also do not consciously register the discrepancies that occur in mirroring.

The brain of both men and women are programmed in different ways to express emotions through body language and facial expressions. The average woman makes use of an average of six primary facial expressions during a listening period of ten seconds to reflect and give feedback on the emotions of the speaker. The face of the woman is likely to mirror the emotions that are expressed by the speaker and if you were watching, you would wonder if the emotion was expressed by the two people.

The woman also reads the meaning of what the speaker is trying to convey by paying attention to their tone of voice and emotional condition through the body language exhibited. Majority of men are daunted by the idea of using facial feedbacks while listening, however, it has several advantages for people who are good at it.

Some men believe that it is "effeminate" to pay attention to facial expressions and feedbacks, however, research using these techniques has shown that when a man mirrors the facial expressions of a woman while she talks, the woman describes such man as being attractive, intelligent, interesting and caring.

On the other hand, men are able to make only fewer than a third of the facial expressions a woman is able to make. Men are used to holding expressionless faces, especially when they are in public, probably because of the evolutionary need to withhold emotion in order to avoid possible attack from strangers and also to appear to be in charge of their emotions. It is for this reason that most men look like statues when they listen to others. This, however, does not mean that men are unable to feel emotions. Brain scans have proven that men are able to experience emotions as strongly as women can, they only refrain from showing it in public.

Looking Alike

People

People tend to look alike when they live together for a long time and also have a good and working relationship. This happens because they constantly mirror the facial expressions of one another, and over time, these mirroring activities build muscle definition in the same areas of their faces. Even couples who are not similar facially can appear similar in a photograph because of their similar smile.

In 2000, Dr. John Gottman of the University of Washington, Seattle along with his colleagues discovered that marriages where one partner does not mirror the other partner's expressions of happiness and instead show expressions of contempt, are more likely to fail, since this behavior exhibited by the partner showing expressions of contempt affect the smiling partner even when they are not consciously aware of what is going on.

Pets

Mirroring also occurs in the pets we choose. Without realizing it, we tend to (unconsciously) favor pets that resemble us physically or appears to reflect our behavior. However, be careful not to presume that our model of body language and social interpretation is the same as that of the dog.

Monkey See, Monkey Do

When you attend a social function or go to a place where people interact, you may want to notice the number of people, who have assumed identical gestures and posture of the person they are communicating with. Mirroring refers to the way one person informs another that he agrees with their ideas and attitudes. Mirroring occur among friends, or between people of similar status. You could also see married couple stand, sit, move and walk in similar manners. Albert Scheflen found that people who are strangers to each other studiously avoid being in mirror positions.

Matching Voices

Intonation, the speed of talking, voice infection, and accents also synchronize during the process of mirroring in order to establish bonding and mutual attitudes further. This is known as pacing and it can seem as if the two people are singing in tune. As a relationship grows over time, the mirroring or the main body language positions reduces as each individual begins to anticipate the behavior of the other person and vocal pacing with the other person becomes the primary way by which the bond can be maintained.

Ensure that you do not speak at a faster rate than the other person does. This is because research has shown that other people feel "pressured" when someone speaks more rapidly than they do. The speed of speech of an individual is an indication of the rate at which the individual is able to analyze information unconsciously. Try to speak at the same rate as the other person or even slightly slower and mirror their intonation and infection.

Who mirrors whom?

Research has shown that when the leader of a group assumes certain postures and exhibit certain gestures, the subordinates are prone to mirror him or her. Leaders are often the first in a group to walk through a doorway. They also like to sit at the end of a table, a sofa, or bench rather than in the middle. When people walk in a room, the person with the highest authority sits at the head of the table, often farthest away from the door, then the subordinates sit in order of their importance within the group.

Steps to mirroring successfully

When it is properly done, mirroring can help to build rapport and maintain a strong bond with other people. The following include ways in which mirroring can be done properly

Building your connection first.

If nothing else, pay attention to this point. "The key to establishing a bond and a strong connection is to first feel the connection yourself. If you are not feeling it, then they are not feeling it." The following describes how to build a strong connection:

Fronting. To begin with, you may want to give the other person your undivided attention. Start by facing the other person, front them so that you are directly facing them. They need to literally be the center of your universe. Focus your complete attention on them.

Eye-contact. When you give too little eye-contact, you may be seen tentative, and when you give too much eye-contact, you may seem creepy. Go for the middle ground. This is going to demonstrate your level of interest in the other person through the complete attention you are paying them. According to Keratin Uväs-Moberg, making eye contact leads to the release of oxytocin, which is the hormone that creates warm feelings that course through us when we are making a close connection.

Triple Nod. The triple nod functions in two important ways. First, research has shown that when you do the triple nod, the person you are communicating with will speak three to four times longer, because they feel listened to and important. Secondly, when we nod, we are essentially agreeing with what other people are saying, thereby building what scientists call a "yes set." This is similar to when you are asked questions such as "Is it still raining?", or "It is indeed warm today, isn't it?" You say yes to these questions (even if only in your mind), research has however shown that once you begin saying yes, then it is more likely that you continue to do so. Yes, set helps to build connections, so every time you nod, you build your yes set, which further strengthens the connection you are trying to create.

Pretend, then Stop Pretending. At this point, you are already fronting the person, making appropriate eye-contact and doing the triple nod. You are probably already feeling a strong connection, however, in order to complete it, you have to make use of the power of your imagination. You can do this by pretending that the individual you are talking to is the most interesting person in your life. Imagine it, and act like it were true. Then, stop pretending.

Mirroring should occur on its own throughout the above procedures, however, there are some other mirroring techniques that will help amplify the bond.

Pace and Volume.

Several times, people think of mirroring as mimicking physical actions, however, mirroring mimics all nonverbal behaviors. You can start with the pace and volume of the speech of the person you are communicating with. If they are loud and they talk super-fast, you will have to increase your animation and volume. However, if they are slow and relaxed, you will also have to match this level and reduce your speed of speech and volume. Matching pace and volume is relatively easy to do and it is less obvious to participate in than the mirroring of physical behaviors.

Identify their punctuator

When you pay careful and adequate attention to another person for a while, you are bound to notice one of the punctuators the person favors., in a bid to get his or her point across. It could be a range of things, such as an eyebrow flash (quick raise of the eyebrows) or some form of hand gestures used by politicians. The following includes an instance of using a punctuator.

"Earlier in the month, while James was having lunch with a psychologist who was to make a pitch concerning private, public and institutional practices., he noticed that when the psychologist was adamant about an issue, in particular, he would bring both of his hands to the front of his body and thrust them up and down vigorously. As he spoke, James prompted him on by nodding at the right time, and smiling when he should. When he, however, came to his conclusion, James mimicked the gesture he had made earlier with both hands. He then stopped, looked at James, cocked his head and said "Yes! You do understand it all!" and he smiled."

The thing however is; James did not say a word. He only made certain gestures and also, he mirrored his gestures.

Testing the Connection

This last part is optional, however, if you desire to test your connection, you should make an overt action that is not related to the conversation and see if it is mirrored back. For example, during the course of a conversation, you may try to scratch your head or itch your nose in order to see if it is mirrored back.

It is however essential that only positive nonverbals should be mirrored and nothing negative. The negative acts could include, closing your eyes and looking away, blocking with your arms folded and turning away etc.

Mirroring body language is an excellent way to establish bonds with people. It is also effective in building trust and understanding people quickly, which in turn makes it easier for you to read people and analyze them.

The secret to building charisma

Have you ever wondered about what it is about some people that makes them so likable?

Irrespective of the personality, there are certain traits that some people exhibit that makes them seem more trustworthy, magnetic and influential. The reason for the above is because they possess charisma.

Charisma is not a trait you are born with; it is one you learn. You can also learn to be charismatic, all you require is to make some modifications to your behavior. Charisma is essentially about what you say and do, and not your mind or person. Everything about you is involved in the development of your charisma ranging from your subconscious to the way you treat others to your physical expressions, your social cues and much more

There are certain things about charismatic people that makes them seem to command a room even without their trying to. People are drawn to them and they want to feed off their vibrant personalities. To put it simply, charismatic people are charming, because charisma makes you likable. It is essential to keep in mind that in order to become charismatic, you need to be a little brave because it is a process that involves looking at the things you do beneath a microscope, it is possible that you do not like what you see, but beating yourself up about it is not the answer. If you, however, keep your expectations in check, you should be able to identify the attitudes and behavior you need to modify.

It is important that you remember that you are only changing the way you are perceived by people and not the kind of person you are. You are only fine-tuning the way you communicate with the world.

Talk about your Passion

It is important to note that the topics you discuss affect your energy level. When you talk about the right topic, it gives power to your voice and it increases your energy level. However, if you think something is boring, it is bound to reduce your energy level substantially. When you talk about a passion of yours: the challenge and things that make you lay awake at night, such as the way you want to impact the world positively, the people you care about and so on, your energy will come through for you. The things you are passionate about will remove fear or nerves from your voice and it will lend you conviction band persuade other people to support you.

Practice Effective Eye Contact

When you practice proper eye contact, you are expressing that you are paying attention, that you care and that you accept the other person as you would accept you (as an individual). When you look down or shift your eye gaze, it shows that you are not interested and your focus is somewhere else.

Practicing eye contact can also be tricky though. When it is too much, you are putting the person off, the same thing applies to when it is too little. In order to know the exact amount, you may have to conduct an experiment. You can do this by trying to maintain eye contact a little longer than you are used to. The way you feel and the reaction of the other person is what you will use to ascertain how long to maintain eye contact. You can practice it on your barista, waiter etc.

After a period of time, you are going to get a feel of what is too much, too little and just enough. How you make eye contact is however dependent on how long the eye contact lasts. If you are not sure of how to start without feeling like a creep, then concentrate on the eye color of the person you are talking to and make a habit of it. This type of eye contact makes you seem personable without being weird.

Be expressive with your Body

There are several ways by which charismatic people express how they feel and using your body in order to emphasize the way you feel or talk about it can go a long way. No one thinks someone who is stiff and rigid is interesting, likable or magnetic. Above all, remember to smile. People who smile are more likable and approachable than people who do not. If you do not know where to begin with your physical expressions, then think of people or pets and notice their physicality.

Also, be aware of the bad forms of expressive behavior. For instance, if you nod your head, it is an excellent way of showing you are listening, however, if you nod it too much, it can look worse than not nodding at all. People are able to pick up on even the slightest expressions you make, so it is essential that you are aware of your biggest offending behaviors. If you are however not sure of what you do poorly ask your friends o someone you trust enough to be honest with you.

Stop for a while and focus on the feeling in your toes. That should give you an overall assessment of all the things your body is doing. "Do you slouch?" "Does your hand fiddle with things in your pocket?" Become aware of these practices and try to adjust.

When in doubt, Practice mirroring

If you want to be charismatic at a particular moment, mirroring qualities is the easiest way to do this. Try to match the physical mannerisms and energy level of other people, and notice how well they are going to respond to it. You do not necessarily have to agree with all the things they say or do, all you need to do is act the way they do in some areas.

You can do this naturally, depending on the social setting, however, it is an easy way of increasing your likability.

You can mirror the qualities you admire in other people too and when it comes to charisma, observation is an important factor. It is important to look to the people you find charismatic. You do not need to copy them, however, learn their secrets, practice them on yourself and fine-tune them until they become a part of you. It is a trial and error process.

Look around you and notice the way people, especially the charismatic ones carry themselves Although, a good number of them might be full of themselves, however, you can like the effective qualities that makes them charismatic for yourself. Try to emulate the people you identify as likable and magnetic and you will find that you will learn certain things as regards how to become more likable.

Admit when you fail

The incredibly successful people of this world are often assumed to have charisma, this has much to do with the fact that they are successful. Their success seems to create a halo effect that is like a glow around them. You do not have to be incredibly successful before you can be extremely charismatic. If you scratch the shiny surface of these successful people, you will find that several of them have the charisma of a rock, they can be so rigid.

However, to become incredibly charismatic, you have to be genuine. You also have to admit when you fail, admit when you make mistakes. Being humble is one of the few traits associated with charisma.

Admit your mistakes and make sure to learn your lesson. Also make it a habit to laugh at yourself when you feel the need to because when you do, people will not laugh at you, they will laugh with you. And they are going to like you better for it.

Do not discuss the failings of others

Maybe all of us likes hearing a little gossip, or a little dirt on people. The problem, however, is that we do not necessarily like the people who dish the dirt and we definitely do not respect them. When people fail or make mistakes, or when you are privy to dirty details concerning them, do not laugh, because when you do, the people around you may wonder if you do the same thing at them. And remember that no one is immune to mistakes. They may also wonder if you would do the same thing to them if they failed or made mistakes. This reduces your likability.

Choose your attitudes and your words carefully

The words you use influence the attitudes of other people and it affects even yourself. For instance, you do not *have to* go to the meeting, you only *get to* go to meet up and interact with other people. You do not *have to* create a presentation for your new client, you only *get to* share some of your cool stuff with other people. Also, you do not *have to* go to the gym, you only *get to* work out and improve your physical fitness. You do not *have to* interview job candidates, you only *get to* select a great person and add him or her to your team.

We all will like to be associated with happy and enthusiastic people, however, the attitudes, words and the approach you employ can make other people feel better about themselves and about you. It can also make you feel better about yourself.

Conquer the Basics of Conversation

Charismatic people know how to communicate with people. They know how and when to start a conversation, they know how to steer it in the right direction and how to make other people feel relaxed. If you do not know how to talk to people on basic levels, you will need to practice it. It is however tough, but if you can be brave and drop the wallflower mentality, then you will be rewarded. At first, practicing may seem uncomfortable, however, that is the only way you can get comfortable. If you have no idea of how to begin a conversation, then get creative. First, ask yourself the things you would like to talk about and things you do not like. It is also much easier if you try to be nice during the conversation than to sound brilliant. Also, note that being nice is a great charisma booster. Just do whatever you can to avoid awkward silence.

Good conversationalists are able to get people on the same level. They are able to tell stories and share experiences. You can also make use of humor during the course of conversing. Meanwhile, remember that humor is not necessarily about what you say, but about how you say it. If you are not sure about the joke, do not tell it. No one will be worse off if you do not tell. If you, however, make a mess of it, it would be awkward and it would suck your charisma. Although, if you tell it right and confidently, it will boost your charisma. When humor is used appropriately, it is able to make you the most likable person in the room.

Finally, make sure to ask questions. People like to be heard, and asking questions give them that opportunity and you, the opportunity to be likable.

Develop a Sense of Confidence

Possessing enough confidence in yourself is going to give you a huge foothold on your way to becoming more charismatic. However, confidence is not easy to build. Confidence is different from arrogance, and you cannot be arrogant if you want to be charismatic. You also do not want to be perceived as timid or scared. It all comes down to how you feel being in your own skin. Certain activities can, however, help you build and maintain confidence. They include working out regularly, talking about the things you understand as well as dressing in clothes that make you feel good, amongst others.

You should, however, not talk about the things you know alone, you should also be open with others and let them know that you are curious while appearing confident. Several people get locked up when they are caught up in conversations that include things they know nothing about, instead of accepting their ignorance and being okay with it, they go on looking for ways to defend themselves. If you shift from being defensive to being curious, you will appear confident even though you do not know anything about the topic of discussion.

Also, being curious helps you maintain interest which is important since you are not drifting off in your mind in the search for answers, you are therefore visibly involved in the conversation.

People with confidence and charisma have a purpose for living. us especially noticeable when you lack a driving force or mission. It does not necessitate you wearing your passion on your sleeve, it only requires you to be confident in the notion that you have a driving factor and mission.

You may not always know where you are headed to, and that is fine, but you should act as you do. It is similar to forgetting your lines in a play, but you act as you know them. Everyone has moments where they take certain actions and they think "that was very stupid," the only thing to do is to forget those moments, because if you think of them longer than is necessary, your behavior may visibly change, and you may visibly falter. Confidence is essentially about being okay with who you are and the actions you take irrespective of what they mean. If you can be confident, being charismatic is not so far away.

Master the Art of Presence

Presence is perhaps the most important aspect of charisma, after which comes confidence, close behind. Presence is essentially about being truly involved with others. You are showing the other person that you are totally engaged with them and that they have your undivided attention. Without confidence, you may be perceived by others as a shy person or someone who is uninterested in others. However, without presence, you can be perceived as someone who is only interested in showing off. Neither extreme happens to be ideal. The art of Presence is about the most importing thing when you are building charisma and that is: It is not about you. It is not about making yourself seem awesome to other people. It is not about your excellent attributes. It is essentially about making other people feel good about themselves.

The truth about human beings is we like ourselves and we enjoy talking about ourselves, and that is the thing with people with charisma. They allow you to tone yourself and talk about yourself. If you want to be charismatic and likable, then be positive, shut down your ego (and mouth) and give the other person your complete attention.

Pay attention to all the words that are being said by other people other. Think of it like you are reading a book or seeing a movie and you are slowly learning about the main character. Focus on them. Most importantly, do not sit there and think about the things you are going to say while they talk to you. Although, it might seem like the proactive thing to do, however, it only shows that you are not paying attention to them, that you are only preparing to retort.

There is however a balance to seek, and that includes the fact that you cannot sit down and listen to people every day and every night. It is important that you, also have to be able to talk and express yourself to other people in a confident manner.

Conclusion

Reading people is a very important skill for anybody to have. This is because it will allow you to understand the complete message somebody is passing across when you are having a conversation with said person. This will put you ahead in your dealings with people and help establish you as a force to reckon with. Humans for a fact say more nonverbally than they do verbally which is why if you are to truly grasp what someone is communicating, you should be able to read and understand their nonverbal communication.

Listening to nonverbal communication is an art that requires training to develop. This particular means of communication, as you now know, says and hints at much more than you are liable to hear and get from having an oral or written conversation with somebody. For instance, body movement can be used to communicate a message in four different ways.

Being adept at the art of nonverbal communication requires that you master some five principles. These principles will not only allow you to identify nonverbal cues, but it will also help interpret them correctly. Without mastery of these principles, you will be prone to make mistakes where reading people is concerned.

Being a master nonverbal communicator also requires that you constantly work on yourself. For instance, emotional awareness, attentiveness and constant practice among others are certain areas that you need to work on and strengthen if you are to become adept at reading what people are saying nonverbally.

Nonverbal communication has a host of benefits some of which are;

- to complement what is being communicated verbally,
- to deceive others into thinking something other than what you feel,

- to regulate what you are communicating verbally,
- to communicate your feelings and emotions on a particular subject and about a particular person,
- and so on.

Another important thing you need to do when developing your nonverbal communication skills is an understanding of personality types. This will enable you to identify the motives behind people's actions which will allow you to understand what it is they are saying.

While being good at reading people is a great skill set, combining this with charisma is even better. This will enable you to resonate with people, empathize and build great rapport with them. All of these are essential especially if you are someone passionate about helping people become the best version of themselves.

Speed reading people is especially important if you are a leader, a politician or somebody who has a job that involves dealing with people. As such, it is important that you learn and develop the skills necessary to become a good reader of people and nonverbal communication. This will put you in a good position to handle people and negotiate with them.

Made in the USA
Middletown, DE
03 August 2019